LITTLE PUFFERS

A Guide to Britain's Narrow Gauge Railways 2008-2009

EDITOR
John Robinson

Fourth Edition

FOREWORD

Following the exceptional success of prior editions of Little Puffers, we have now moved all the miniature railways (which we define as being of 7¼ inch gauge and less) into 'Tiny Trains', the 2nd edition of which is being published at the same time as this guide.

British Library Cataloguing in Publication Data
A catalogue record for this book is available from the British Library

ISBN-13: 978-1-86223-165-8

Manufactured in the UK by LPPS Ltd, Wellingborough, NN8 3PJ

ACKNOWLEDGEMENTS

We were greatly impressed by the friendly and cooperative manner of the staff and helpers of the railways which we selected to appear in this book, and wish to thank them all for the help they have given. In addition we wish to thank Bob Budd (cover design) and Michael Robinson (page layouts) for their help.

We are particularly indebted to Keith Watson and Peter Bryant for their invaluable assistance. Peter's web site: www.miniaturerailwayworld.co.uk provides a great deal of information about Narrow Gauge and Miniature Railways in the UK.

Although we believe that the information contained in this guide is accurate at the time of going to press, we, and the Railways and Museums itemised, are unable to accept liability for any loss, damage, distress or injury suffered as a result of any inaccuracies. Furthermore, we and the Railways are unable to guarantee operating and opening times which may always be subject to cancellation without notice.

If you feel we should include other locations or information in future editions, please let us know so that we may give them consideration. We would like to thank you for buying this guide and wish you 'Happy Railway Travelling'!

John Robinson

EDITOR

Note: Further copies of Little Puffers, Still Steaming and Tiny Trains, can be ordered, post free, from our address shown on the left or on-line via our web site –

www.stillsteaming.com

RAILWAY LOCATOR MAP

The numbers shown on this map relate to the page numbers for each railway. Pages 6-8 contain an alphabetical listing of the railways featured in this guide. Please note that the markers on this map show the approximate location only.

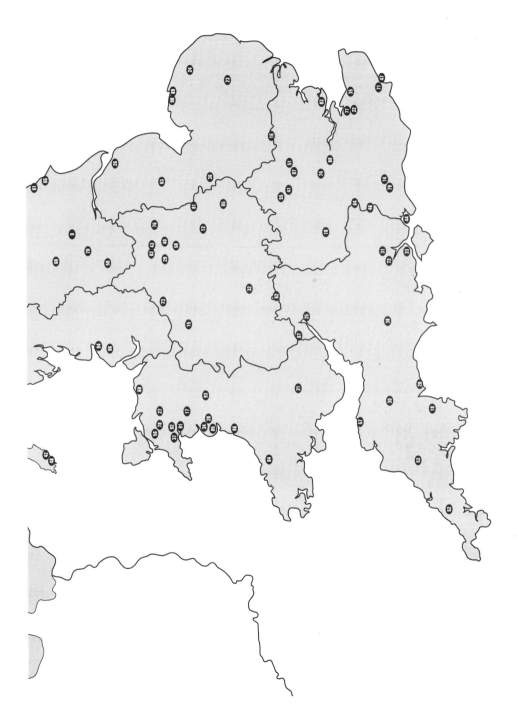

CONTENTS

NATIONAL RAILWAY MUSEUM

Address: National Railway Museum, Leeman Road, York YO26 4XJ **Telephone Nº**: 08448 153139 **Year Formed**: 1975 **Location of Line**: York **Length of Line**: Short demonstration line	**Nº of Steam Locos**: 79 **Nº of Other Locos**: 37 **Approx Nº of Visitors P.A.**: 800,000 **Web site**: www.nrm.org.uk

GENERAL INFORMATION

Nearest Mainline Station: York (¼ mile)
Nearest Bus Station: York (¼ mile)
Car Parking: On site long stay car park
Coach Parking: On site – free to pre-booked groups
Souvenir Shop(s): Yes
Food & Drinks: Yes

SPECIAL INFORMATION

The Museum is the largest of its kind in the world, housing the Nation's collection of locomotives, carriages, uniforms, posters and an extensive photographic archive. Special events and exhibitions run throughout the year. The Museum is the home of the Mallard – the fastest steam locomotive in the world and Shinkansen, the only Bullet train outside of Japan.

OPERATING INFORMATION

Opening Times: Open daily 10.00am to 6.00pm (closed on 24th, 25th and 26th of December)
Steam Working: School holidays – please phone to confirm details
Prices: Free admission for all (excludes some Special events)
Please phone 08448 153139 for further details.

Detailed Directions by Car:
The Museum is located in the centre of York, just behind the Railway Station. It is clearly signposted from all approaches to York.

Shildon is one of the world's oldest railway towns and was selected by the National Railway Museum as a site for Locomotion, the first national museum to be built in the North East. The new building houses the reserve collection of historically important railway vehicles and these are now accessible to the public for the first time.

Shildon was home to the Timothy Hackworth Museum with its workshops and historic buildings and the incorporation of these with the new Locomotion museum creates an exciting opportunity to discover the significance of Shildon in railway history.

The replica Sans Pareil locomotive pictured below gives rides during the Summer School Holidays and on other special event days.

LOCOMOTION – THE NATIONAL RAILWAY MUSEUM AT SHILDON

Address: Locomotion, Shildon, County Durham   DL14 1PQ
Telephone Nº: (01388) 777999
Fax Nº: (01388) 771448
Year Formed: 2004
Location: Shildon, County Durham

Length of Line: Over ½ mile
Nº of Steam Locos: 60 locomotives and other rail vehicles
Approx Nº of Visitors P.A.: 60,000+
Gauge: Standard
Web site: www.locomotion.uk.com

GENERAL INFORMATION

Nearest Mainline Station: Shildon (adjacent)
Nearest Bus Station: Durham
Car Parking: Available on site
Coach Parking: Available on site
Souvenir Shop(s): Yes
Food & Drinks: Yes

SPECIAL INFORMATION

This extensive site is the first regional branch of the National Railway Museum and houses vehicles from the National Collection in a purpose-built 6,000 square-foot building.

OPERATING INFORMATION

Opening Times: Daily from 17th March to 5th October 2008 – 10.00am to 5.00pm. Also open from Wednesday to Sunday during the Winter season – 6th October to 1st April from 10.00am to 4.00pm although the Museum is closed over the Christmas and New Year Holiday period.
Steam Working: During the Summer School Holidays and on special event days – please phone to confirm details.
Prices: Admission to the Museum is free of charge.
Train Rides: Adults £1.50
                        Concessions 75p

Detailed Directions by Car:
From All Parts: Exit the A1(M) at Junction 58 and take the A68 and the A6072 to Shildon. Follow the Brown tourist signs to Locomotion which is situated ¼ mile to the south-east of the Town Centre.

ABBEY PUMPING STATION

Address: Abbey Pumping Station Museum, Corporation Road, Leicester, LE4 5PX **Telephone N°:** (0116) 299-5111 **Year Formed:** 1980s **Location of Line:** Leicester **Length of Line:** 300 yards	**N° of Steam Locos:** 1 **N° of Other Locos:** 4 **N° of Members:** Approximately 80 **Annual Membership Fee:** £8.00 Adult, £10.00 Family **Approx N° of Visitors P.A.:** 60,000 **Gauge:** 2 feet

GENERAL INFORMATION

Nearest Mainline Station: Leicester London Road (3 miles)
Nearest Bus Station: Leicester (1½ miles)
Car Parking: Free parking available on site
Coach Parking: Use the Space Centre car park
Souvenir Shop(s): Yes
Food & Drinks: Available on special event days only

SPECIAL INFORMATION

The Museum is situated in the Abbey Pumping Station which, from 1891 to 1964 pumped Leicester's sewage to nearby treatment works. The Museum now collects and displays the industrial, technological and scientific heritage of Leicester and contains rare working examples of Woolf compound rotative beam engines which are in steam on selected days.

OPERATING INFORMATION

Opening Times: Monday to Wednesday and weekends from the beginning of February to the end of November. Open 11.00am – 4.30pm on weekdays and Saturdays and 1.00pm – 4.30pm on Sundays.
Steam Working: Selected special event days only. 2008 dates: 3rd May; 7th, 28th & 29th June; 5th July; 2nd August; 6th September; 4th & 18th October; 7th December. Contact the Museum for further details.
Prices: Adults £3.50 (Special event days only)
Concessions £2.00 (Special events only)
Family £8.00 (Special event days only)

Detailed Directions by Car:
From All Parts: The Museum is situated next to the National Space Centre, about 1 mile North of Leicester city centre near Beaumont Leys and Belgrave. Brown tourist signs with a distinctive rocket logo provide directions to the NSC from the arterial routes around Leicester and the Museum is nearby.

ALFORD VALLEY RAILWAY

Address: Alford Station, Main Street, Alford, Aberdeenshire AB33 8HH	**Nº of Steam Locos**: None at present
Telephone Nº: (07879) 293934	**Nº of Other Locos**: 3
Year Formed: 1980	**Nº of Members**: Approximately 30
Location of Line: Alford – Haughton Park	**Annual Membership Fee**: £6.00
Length of Line: 1 mile	**Approx Nº of Visitors P.A.**: 19,500
	Gauge: 2 feet
	Web site: www.alfordvalleyrailway.org.uk

GENERAL INFORMATION

Nearest Mainline Station: Insch (10 miles)
Nearest Bus Station: Alford (200 yards)
Car Parking: Available on site
Coach Parking: Available on site
Souvenir Shop(s): Yes
Food & Drinks: No

SPECIAL INFORMATION

The Grampian Transport Museum is adjacent to the Railway and the Heritage Centre also has horse-drawn tractors and agricultural machinery.

OPERATING INFORMATION

Opening Times: Weekends in April, May and September. Open daily in June, July and August. Trains usually run from 1.00pm to 4.30pm but from 10.30am to 2.30pm on weekdays in June.
Steam Working: None at present
Prices: Adult Return £2.50
        Child Return £1.00

Detailed Directions by Car:

From All Parts: Alford is situated 25 miles west of Aberdeen on the Highland tourist route. Take the A944 to reach Alford.

AMBERLEY WORKING MUSEUM

Address: Amberley Working Museum, Amberley, Arundel BN18 9LT	**Nº of Steam Locos**: 3
Telephone Nº: (01798) 831370	**Nº of Other Locos**: 20+
Year Formed: 1979	**Nº of Members**: 300 volunteers
Location of Line: Amberley	**Annual Membership Fee**: £22.00
Length of Line: ¾ mile	**Approx Nº of Visitors P.A.**: 60,000
	Gauge: 2 feet
	Web site: www.amberleymuseum.co.uk

GENERAL INFORMATION

Nearest Mainline Station: Amberley (adjacent)
Nearest Bus Station: –
Car Parking: Free parking available on site
Coach Parking: Free parking available on site
Souvenir Shop(s): Yes
Food & Drinks: Yes

SPECIAL INFORMATION

Amberley Working Museum covers 36 acres of former chalk pits and consists of over 30 buildings containing hundreds of different exhibits.

The Railway is holding its annual Gala weekend on 12th and 13th July 2008.

OPERATING INFORMATION

Opening Times: Wednesday to Sunday from 16th February to 2nd November 2008 and also on Bank Holidays. Trains run from 10.00am to 5.30pm
Steam Working: Please phone for details.
Prices: Adult £9.30
Child £5.80 (free for Under-5's)
Family £26.50 (2 adults + 3 children)

Detailed Directions by Car:
From All Parts: Amberley Working Museum is situated in West Sussex on the B2139 mid-way between Arundel and Storrington and is adjacent to Amberley Railway Station.

AMERTON RAILWAY

Address: Amerton Farm, Stow-by-Chartley, Staffordshire   ST18 0LA
Telephone Nº: (01785) 850965
Year Formed: 1991
Location: Amerton Farm
Length of Line: Approximately 1 mile

Nº of Steam Locos: 2
Nº of Other Locos: 7
Nº of Members: 45
Approx Nº of Visitors P.A.: 30,000
Gauge: 2 feet
Web site: www.amertonrailway.co.uk

GENERAL INFORMATION

Nearest Mainline Station: Stafford (8 miles)
Nearest Bus Station: Stafford (8 miles)
Car Parking: Free parking available on site
Coach Parking: Available by arrangement
Souvenir Shop(s): Yes
Food & Drinks: Yes

SPECIAL INFORMATION

The Railway is run by volunteers and the circuit was completed in 2002. The Summer Steam Gala will be held on 14th & 15th June.

OPERATING INFORMATION

Opening Times: Weekends from the end of March to the end of October and on Tuesdays & Thursdays during School Holidays. Also open for Santa Specials in December. Open from midday to 5.00pm
Steam Working: Sundays and Bank Holidays only.
Prices: Adult £1.80
     Child £1.20
     Concession £1.50

Detailed Directions by Car:
Amerton is located on the A518, 1 mile from the junction with the A51 – Amerton Farm is signposted at the junction. The Railway is located approximately 8 miles from Junction 14 of the M6.

AUDLEY END STEAM RAILWAY

Address: Audley End, Saffron Walden, Essex **Telephone Nº**: (01799) 541354 **Year Formed**: 1964 **Location of Line**: Opposite Audley End House, Saffron Walden	**Length of Line**: 1½ miles **Nº of Steam Locos**: 6 **Nº of Other Locos**: 3 **Nº of Members**: None **Approx Nº of Visitors P.A.**: 42,000 **Gauge**: 10¼ inches **Web site**: www.audley-end-railway.co.uk

GENERAL INFORMATION

Nearest Mainline Station: Audley End (1 mile)
Nearest Bus Station: Saffron Walden (1 mile)
Car Parking: Available on site
Coach Parking: Available on site
Souvenir Shop(s): Yes
Food & Drinks: Snacks available

SPECIAL INFORMATION

Audley End Steam Railway is Lord Braybrooke's private miniature railway situated just next to Audley End House, an English Heritage site. Private parties can be catered for outside of normal running hours.

OPERATING INFORMATION

Opening Times: Weekends from 17th March to the end of October and also daily during School Holidays. Also Santa Specials in December. Trains run from 2.00pm (11.00am on Bank Holidays).
Steam Working: Sundays only
Prices: Adult Return £3.00
 Child Return £2.00
 Santa Specials £4.00

Detailed Directions by Car:
Exit the M11 at Junction 10 if southbound or Junction 9 if northbound and follow the signs for Audley End House. The railway is situated just across the road from Audley End House.

BALA LAKE RAILWAY

Address: Bala Lake Railway, Llanuwchllyn, Gwynedd, LL23 7DD **Telephone Nº**: (01678) 540666 **Year Formed**: 1972 **Location of Line**: Llanuwchllyn to Bala **Length of Line**: 4½ miles	**Nº of Steam Locos**: 5 (all are not in **Nº of Other Locos**: 3 working order) **Nº of Members**: – **Approx Nº of Visitors P.A.**: 20,000 **Gauge**: 1 foot 11 five-eighth inches **Web site**: www.bala-lake-railway.co.uk

GENERAL INFORMATION

Nearest Mainline Station: Wrexham (40 miles)
Nearest Bus Station: Wrexham (40 miles)
Car Parking: Adequate parking in Llanuwchllyn
Coach Parking: At Llanuwchllyn or in Bala Town Centre
Souvenir Shop(s): Yes
Food & Drinks: Yes – unlicensed!

SPECIAL INFORMATION

Bala Lake Railway is a narrow-gauge railway which follows 4½ miles of the former Ruabon to Barmouth G.W.R. line.

OPERATING INFORMATION

Opening Times: Easter until the end of September closed on Mondays and Fridays (excepting Bank Holidays) in April, May, June and September.
Steam Working: All advertised services are steam hauled. Trains run from 11.15am to 4.00pm.
Prices: Adult Single £5.00;   Return £7.50
              Child Single £2.00;   Return £3.00
              Senior Citizen Return £7.00
Family Tickets (Return): £9.00 (1 Adult + 1 Child); £18.00 (2 Adults + 2 Children). Additional Children are £2.00 each.
Under 5's and dogs travel free of charge!

Detailed Directions by Car:
From All Parts: The railway is situated off the A494 Bala to Dolgellau road which is accessible from the national motorways via the A5 or A55.

BEALE RAILWAY

Address: Beale Park, Lower Basildon, Pangbourne RG8 9NH	**N of Steam Locos**: 1
	N of Other Locos: 1
Telephone N: 0870 777-7160	**Approx N of Visitors P.A.**: –
Year Formed: 1989	**Gauge**: 10¼ inches
Location of Line: Pangbourne, Berks.	**Web site**: www.bealepark.co.uk
Length of Line: Approximately 1 mile	

GENERAL INFORMATION

Nearest Mainline Station: Pangbourne (1 mile)
Nearest Bus Station: Reading (12 miles)
Car Parking: Available on site
Coach Parking: Available on site
Souvenir Shop(s): Yes
Food & Drinks: Available

SPECIAL INFORMATION

The railway is situated within Child-Beale Trust, Beale Park alongside the River Thames. The Park has numerous other attractions including collections of small exotic animals, farm animals & birds, landscaped gardens & woodlands and play areas.

OPERATING INFORMATION

Opening Times: Beale Park is open daily from the 1st March to 31st October. Open from 10.00am to 5.00pm in March and October and until 6.00pm at other times. The first train departs at 10.30am daily and the last train departs 15 minutes before Beale Park closes.

Steam Working: Trains may be steam or diesel-hauled depending on operational needs.

Prices: One free ride is included in the park admission fee. All rides thereafter are £1.00 each.

Park Admission: Adults £6.00 or £8.00
Children £4.00 or £5.50
Senior Citizens £4.50 or £6.50

Note: The lower prices shown above are valid only for March and October. The higher prices shown are charged between April and September.

Detailed Directions by Car:
Beale Park is situated just off the A329 Reading to Goring Road at Pangbourne.

BICKINGTON STEAM RAILWAY

Address: Trago Mills Shopping & Leisure Centre, Stover, Devon TQ12 6JB **Telephone Nº**: (01626) 821111 **Year Formed**: 1988 **Location of Line**: Near the junction of A38 and A382 **Length of Line**: 1½ miles	**Nº of Steam Locos**: 4 **Nº of Other Locos**: 1 **Nº of Members**: None **Approx Nº of Visitors P.A.**: Not known **Gauge**: 10¼ inches **Web site**: None

GENERAL INFORMATION

Nearest Mainline Station: Newton Abbott (3½ miles)
Nearest Bus Station: Newton Abbott
Car Parking: Free parking available on site
Coach Parking: Available on site
Souvenir Shop(s): Yes
Food & Drinks: Available adjacent to the Railway

SPECIAL INFORMATION

Bickington Steam Railway is part of the Trago Mills Shopping & Leisure Centre which occupies around 100 acres of rolling South Devon countryside. The site has numerous other attractions including, 'The Finest 00-gauge Model Railway in the UK'!

OPERATING INFORMATION

Opening Times: Monday to Saturday 11.00am to 5.00pm and Sundays 12.00pm to 4.00pm.
Steam Working: Most operating days but please contact the Railway for precise information.
Prices: £4.99 for a Day Ticket which gives 10 rides.

Detailed Directions by Car:
From All Parts: Take the M5 from Exeter to the A38 and head towards Plymouth. Exit at the junction with the A382 and follow the signs for 'Trago Mills'. The railway is situated on this road after about 1 mile.

BICTON WOODLAND RAILWAY

Address: Bicton Woodland Railway, Bicton Park Botanical Gardens, East Budleigh, Budleigh Salterton EX9 7OP **Telephone Nº**: (01395) 568465 **Year Formed**: 1963 **Location of Line**: Bicton Gardens **Length of Line**: 1½ miles	**Nº of Steam Locos**: None at present **Nº of Other Locos**: 3 **Nº of Members**: 15,000 **Annual Membership Fee**: From £12.00 **Approx Nº of Visitors P.A.**: 300,000 **Gauge**: 1 foot 6 inches **Web site**: www.bictongardens.co.uk

GENERAL INFORMATION

Nearest Railtrack Station: Exmouth (6 miles)
Nearest Bus Station: Exeter (14 miles)
Car Parking: Free parking at site
Coach Parking: Free parking at site
Souvenir Shop(s): Yes
Food & Drinks: Yes

SPECIAL INFORMATION

The railway runs through the grounds of Bicton Park Botanical Gardens which span over 60 acres.

OPERATING INFORMATION

Opening Times: Daily 10.00am to 6.00pm during the Summer and 10.00am to 5.00pm during the Winter. Closed on Christmas Day and Boxing Day.
Steam Working: None at present
Entrance Fee: Adult £6.95
Child/Senior Citizen £5.95
Family £22.95
Note: There is an additional charge of £1.30 per person for train rides. Under-3s ride for free.

Detailed Directions by Car:
From All Parts: Exit the M5 motorway at Exeter services, Junction 30 and follow the brown tourist signs to Bicton Park.

BRECON MOUNTAIN RAILWAY

Address: Pant Station, Dowlais,
Merthyr Tydfil   CF48 2UP
Telephone Nº: (01685) 722988
Year Formed: 1980
Location of Line: North of Merthyr
Tydfil – 1 mile from the A465
Gauge: 1 foot 11¾ inches

Length of Line: 5 miles (3½ in service)
Nº of Steam Locos: 8
Nº of Other Locos: 1
Nº of Members: –
Annual Membership Fee: –
Approx Nº of Visitors P.A.: 75,000
Web site: www.breconmountainrailway.co.uk

GENERAL INFORMATION

Nearest Mainline Station: Merthyr Tydfil (3 miles)
Nearest Bus Station: Merthyr Tydfil (3 miles)
Car Parking: Available at Pant Station
Coach Parking: Available at Pant Station
Souvenir Shop(s): Yes
Food & Drinks: Yes – including licensed restaurant

SPECIAL INFORMATION

It is possible to take a break before the return
journey at Pontsticill to have a picnic, take a forest
walk or visit the lakeside snackbar.

OPERATING INFORMATION

Opening Times: Daily from 21st March to 2nd
November. Closed on some Mondays and Fridays in
April, May, September and October.
Steam Working: 11.00am to 5.15pm
Prices: Adult Return £9.50
Child Return (15 and under) £4.75
Senior Citizen Return £8.75
Dogs or Bicycles £2.00
Family Rate – The first two children can
travel for £3.50 each when accompanied by an adult.

Detailed Directions by Car:
Exit the M4 at Junction 32 and take the A470 to Merthyr Tydfil. Go onto the A465 and follow the brown tourist
signs for the railway.

BREDGAR & WORMSHILL LIGHT RAILWAY

Address: The Warren, Bredgar,
near Sittingbourne, Kent   ME9 8AT
Telephone Nº: (01622) 884254
Year Formed: 1972
Location of Line: 1 mile south of Bredgar
Gauge: 2 feet
Length of Line: ¾ mile

Nº of Steam Locos: 10
Nº of Other Locos: 2
Nº of Members: –
Annual Membership Fee: –
Approx Nº of Visitors P.A.: 7,000
Web site: www.bwlr.co.uk

GENERAL INFORMATION

Nearest Mainline Station:
Hollingbourne (3 miles) or Sittingbourne (5 miles)
Nearest Bus Station: Sittingbourne
Car Parking: 500 spaces available – free parking
Coach Parking: Free parking available by appointment
Souvenir Shop(s): Yes
Food & Drinks: Yes

SPECIAL INFORMATION

A small but beautiful railway in rural Kent. The railway also has other attractions including a Model Railway, Traction Engines, a working Beam Engine, Vintage cars, a Locomotive Shed, a picnic site and woodland walks.

OPERATING INFORMATION

Opening Times: Open on the first Sunday of the month from May to October. Open from 10.30am to 5.00pm
Steam Working: 11.00am to 4.30pm
Prices: Adult £7.50   Child £3.00

Detailed Directions by Car:
Take the M20 and exit at Junction 8 (Leeds Castle exit). Travel 4½ miles due north through Hollingbourne. The Railway is situated a little over 1 mile south of Bredgar village.

BRESSINGHAM STEAM EXPERIENCE

Address: Bressingham Steam Museum, Bressingham, Diss, Norfolk IP22 2AB
Telephone Nº: (01379) 686900
Year Formed: Mid 1950's
Location of Line: Bressingham, Near Diss
Length of Line: 5 miles in total (3 lines)

Nº of Steam Locos: Many Steam locos
Nº of Members: 70 volunteers
Annual Membership Fee: –
Approx Nº of Visitors P.A.: 80,000+
Gauge: Standard, 2 foot, 10¼ inches and 15 inches
Web site: www.bressingham.co.uk

GENERAL INFORMATION

Nearest Mainline Station: Diss (2½ miles)
Nearest Bus Station: Bressingham (1¼ miles)
Car Parking: Free parking for 400 cars available
Coach Parking: Free parking for 30 coaches
Souvenir Shop(s): Yes
Food & Drinks: Yes

SPECIAL INFORMATION

In addition to Steam locomotives, Bressingham has a large selection of steam traction engines, fixed steam engines and also the National Dad's Army Museum, two extensive gardens and a water garden centre.

OPERATING INFORMATION

Opening Times: Daily from 20th March to the 2nd November 2008 from 10.30am to 5.00pm. Open until 5.30pm in June, July and August.
Steam Working: Almost every operating day except for most Mondays and Tuesdays in March, April, May, June, July, September and October. Please contract the Museum for further details.
Prices: Adult £9.50 (non-Steam) £12.00 (Steam)
Child £6.50 (non-Steam) £8.00 (Steam)
Family £26 (non-Steam) £35.00 (Steam)
Seniors £8.50 (non-Steam) £10.50 (Steam)

Detailed Directions by Car:
From All Parts: Take the A11 to Thetford and then follow the A1066 towards Diss for Bressingham. The Museum is signposted by the brown tourist signs.

BURE VALLEY RAILWAY

Address: Aylsham Station, Norwich Road, Aylsham, Norfolk NR11 6BW
Telephone Nº: (01263) 733858
Year Formed: 1989
Location of Line: Between Aylsham and Wroxham
Length of Line: 9 miles

Nº of Steam Locos: 5
Nº of Other Locos: 3
Approx Nº of Visitors P.A.: 120,000
Gauge: 15 inches
Web Site: www.bvrw.co.uk
e-mail: info@bvrw.co.uk

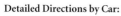

GENERAL INFO

Nearest Mainline Station: Wroxham (adjacent)
Nearest Bus Station: Aylsham (bus passes station)
Car Parking: Free parking at Aylsham & Wroxham Stations
Coach Parking: As above
Souvenir Shop(s): Yes at both Stations
Food & Drinks: Yes (a Restaurant at Aylsham also opens daily)

SPECIAL INFO

Boat trains connect at Wroxham with a 1½ hour cruise on the Norfolk Broads. Steam Locomotive driving courses are available throughout the year except in July and August. Some carriages are able to carry wheelchairs.

OPERATING INFO

Opening Times: Aylsham Station is open daily. Trains run on various dates in 2008 from 9th February to 2nd November. Open during weekends in March, April and October and daily from 25th April to 5th October plus some other dates. Trains run from 9.25am to 6.15pm during high season. Open for Santa Specials on dates in December – phone for further details.
Steam Working:
Most trains are steam hauled
Prices: Adult Return £10.50
(Single £7.00)
Child Return £6.00
(Single £4.50)
Senior Citizen Return £9.50
(Single £6.50)
Family Return £29.00
(2 adult + 2 child)
Party discounts are available for groups of 20 or more if booked in advance.

Detailed Directions by Car:
From Norwich: Aylsham Station is situated midway between Norwich and Cromer on the A140 – follow the signs for Aylsham Town Centre. Wroxham Station is adjacent to the Wroxham British Rail Station – take the A1151 from Norwich; From King's Lynn: Take the A148 and B1354 to reach Aylsham Station.

THE CATTLE COUNTRY RAILWAY

Address: Cattle Country Adventure Park, Berkeley Heath Farm, Berkeley, Glos, GL13 9EW
Telephone Nº: (01453) 810510
Year Formed: 2005
Location of Line: Berkeley Heath
Length of Line: ½ mile

Nº of Steam Locos: None at present
Nº of Other Locos: 1
Approx Nº of Visitors P.A.: 100,000
Gauge: 10¼ inches
Web site: www.cattlecountry.co.uk

GENERAL INFORMATION

Nearest Mainline Station: Cam & Dursley (5 miles)
Car Parking: Free parking available on site
Coach Parking: Free parking available on site
Souvenir Shop(s): Yes
Food & Drinks: Yes

SPECIAL INFORMATION

The railway runs through the Cattle Country Adventure Park which hosts a wide variety of attractions for all the family. Entrance fees to the Park vary depending on the time of the year. Details can be found on: www.cattlecountry.co.uk

OPERATING INFORMATION

Opening Times: Open on Sundays from mid-February to the end of October. Also open on Saturdays from Easter to the end of August, daily from 1st July to 2nd September 2008 and at various other dates. Contact the Park for further details. Open 10.00am to 4.00pm (5.00pm in the Summer).
Steam Working: None at present.
Prices: Adult Return £1.50 (Single £1.00)
Child Return £1.00 (Single 75p)
Note: Admission charges for the Cattle Country Adventure Park are an additional charge.

Detailed Directions by Car:
From the North: Exit the M5 at Junction 13 and join the A38 travelling towards Bristol. After 8 miles you reach Berkeley Heath, turn right past the garage and follow the brown tourist signs for Cattle Country; From the South: Exit the M5 at Junction 14 and take the A38 towards Gloucester. After approximately 6 miles turn left following the brown tourist signs for Cattle Country.

CLEETHORPES COAST LIGHT RAILWAY

Address: King's Road, Cleethorpes,
North East Lincolnshire   DN35 0AG
Telephone Nº: (01472) 604657
Year Formed: 1948
Location of Line: Lakeside Park & Marine
embankment along Cleethorpes seafront
Length of Line: Almost 2 miles

Nº of Steam Locos: 9
Nº of Other Locos: 4
Nº of Members: 65
Annual Membership Fee: Adult £11.00
Approx Nº of Visitors P.A.: 120,000
Gauge: 15 inches
Web: www.cleethorpescoastlightrailway.co.uk

GENERAL INFORMATION

Nearest Mainline Station: Cleethorpes (1 mile)
Nearest Bus Stop: Meridian Point (opposite)
Car Parking: Boating Lake car park – 500 spaces
(fee charged)
Coach Parking: As above
Souvenir Shop(s): Yes
Food & Drinks: Brief Encounters Tearoom on
Lakeside Station

SPECIAL INFORMATION

An line extension to Humberston opens in May 2007.

OPERATING INFORMATION

Opening Times: Open daily from 31st March to
31st October. Open during weekends, Bank holidays
and school holidays at all other times. Open
11.00am to 4.20pm in Winter, 6.00pm in Summer.
Steam Working: Weekends throughout the year and
daily from March to October.
Prices: To be confirmed – please contact the
railway for further details.

Detailed Directions by Car:
Take the M180 to the A180 and continue to its' end. Follow signs for Cleethorpes. The Railway is situated along
Cleethorpes seafront 1 mile south of the Pier. Look for the brown Railway Engine tourist signs and the main
station is adjacent to the Leisure Centre.

CONWY VALLEY RAILWAY MUSEUM

Address: Old Goods Yard, Betws-y-Coed, Conwy, North Wales LL24 0AL **Telephone No**: (01690) 710568 **Year Formed**: 1983 **Location of Line**: Betws-y-Coed **Length of Line**: One and an eighth miles	**No of Steam Locos**: 4 **No of Other Locos**: 2 **No of Members**: – **Annual Membership Fee**: – **Approx No of Visitors P.A.**: 50,000 **Gauge**: 7¼ inches and 15 inches **Web site**: www.conwyrailwaymuseum.co.uk

GENERAL INFORMATION

Nearest Mainline Station: Betws-y-Coed (20 yards)
Nearest Bus Station: 40 yards
Car Parking: Car park at site
Coach Parking: Car park at site
Souvenir Shop(s): Yes
Food & Drinks: Yes – Buffet Coach Cafe

SPECIAL INFORMATION

The Museum houses the unique 3D dioramas by the late Jack Nelson. Also the ¼ size steam loco 'Britannia'. The Railway now has two Isle of Man locos – "Douglas" and "Dragonfly" and a Tinkerbell loco "Petunia" is currently on loan.

OPERATING INFORMATION

Opening Times: Daily from 10.00am to 5.00pm.
Trains Working: Daily from 10.15am
Prices: Adult – £1.50 museum entry;
Train rides £1.50; Tram rides £1.00
Child/Senior Citizen – 80p museum entry;
Train rides £1.50; Tram rides £1.00
Family tickets – £4.00

Detailed Directions by Car:
From Midlands & South: Take M54/M6 onto the A5 and into Betws-y-Coed; From Other Parts: Take the A55 coast road then the A470 to Betws-y-Coed. The museum is located by the Mainline Station directly off the A5.

THE CORRIS RAILWAY

Address: Station Yard, Corris, Machynlleth, Mid Wales SY20 9SH	**Nº of Steam Locos:** 1
Telephone Nº: (01654) 761303	**Nº of Other Locos:** 1
Year Formed: 1966	**Nº of Members:** 500
Location of Line: Corris to Maespoeth, Mid Wales	**Annual Membership Fee:** £15.00 (adult)
	Approx Nº of Visitors P.A.: 7,000
Length of Line: ¾ mile	**Gauge:** 2 feet 3 inches
	Web site: www.corris.co.uk

GENERAL INFORMATION

Nearest Mainline Station: Machynlleth (5 miles)
Nearest Bus Station: Machynlleth (5 miles)
Car Parking: Available on site and also at the Corris Craft Centre (500 yards)
Coach Parking: Corris Craft Centre (please pre-book if visiting)
Souvenir Shop(s): Yes
Food & Drinks: Yes

SPECIAL INFORMATION

The Corris Railway Society was formed in 1966 and the line itself dates back to 1859. The Railway's new-build steam loco was delivered in the Spring of 2005.

OPERATING INFORMATION

Opening Times: Open over the Easter weekend and then every Sunday until 30th September. Also open for the whole of the first and last week in August and various other dates throughout the year. Trains run from 10.30am to 5.00pm.
Steam Working: Please phone for details.
Prices: Adult Return £4.00
         Child/Senior Citizen Return £2.00
         Family Return £10.00
              (2 adults + 2 children)

Detailed Directions by Car:

From All Parts: Corris is situated off the A487 trunk road, five miles north of Machynlleth and 11 miles south of Dolgellau. Turn off the trunk road at the Braichgoch Hotel and the Station Yard is the 2nd turn of the right as you enter the village, just past the Holy Trinity Church.

DERBYSHIRE DALES NARROW GAUGE RAILWAY

Correspondence: 44 Midland Terrace, Westhouses, Alfreton DE55 5AB
Contact Phone N°: (01773) 831209
Year Formed: 1998
Location of Line: Rowsley South Station, Peak Rail
Length of Line: 500 yards

N° of Steam Locos: None
N° of Other Locos: 7
Approx N° of Visitors P.A.: Not known
Gauge: 2 feet
Web site: www.peakrail.co.uk

GENERAL INFORMATION

Nearest Mainline Station: Matlock (4 miles)
Nearest Bus Station: Matlock (4 miles)
Car Parking: 200 spaces at Rowsley South Station
Coach Parking: Free parking at Rowsley South
Souvenir Shop(s): Yes
Food & Drinks: Yes

SPECIAL INFORMATION

This narrow gauge line is operated at Peak Rail's Rowsley South Station. The line has now been extended to 500 yards.

OPERATING INFORMATION

Opening Times: Sundays and Bank Holiday weekends from April to the end of August. Also open on certain other dates – please contact the railway for further information.
Steam Working: None at present.
Prices: Adult £1.00
   Children 25p
Note: One child travels for free with each adult.

Detailed Directions by Car:
Follow the A6 Bakewell to Matlock road to Rowsley then follow the brown tourist signs for the Peak Rail Station.

DEVON RAILWAY CENTRE

Address: Bickleigh, Tiverton, Devon, EX16 8RG	**N° of Steam Locos**: 3
	N° of Other Locos: 15
Telephone N°: (01884) 855671	**N° of Members**: None
Year Formed: 1997	**Approx N° of Visitors P.A.**: –
Location of Line: Bickleigh, Devon	**Gauge**: 2 feet, 7¼ inches and Standard
Length of Line: ½ mile (2 foot and 7¼ inch gauges); 200 yards (Standard gauge)	**Web site**: www.devonrailwaycentre.co.uk

GENERAL INFORMATION

Nearest Mainline Station: Exeter
Nearest Bus Station: Tiverton (Route 55)
Car Parking: Available on site
Coach Parking: Available on site
Souvenir Shop(s): Yes
Food & Drinks: Yes

SPECIAL INFORMATION

Devon Railway Centre has passenger carrying lines and also features a large model railway exhibition with 15 working layouts. A delightful Edwardian model village has recently been built to a 1:12 scale.

OPERATING INFORMATION

Opening Times: Daily 5th–20th April, 21st May to 7th September and 25th October to 2nd November. Closed Mondays in June. Open Wednesday to Friday & Weekends from 7th to 18th May and 10th to 28th September. Open during weekends in October and May Bank Holiday weekend. Open from 10.30am until 5.00pm on each of these days.
Steam Working: Trains may be steam or diesel hauled so please phone for further details.
Prices: Adult £5.80   Child £4.70
      Senior Citizen £4.90   Family £17.80
Admission includes unlimited train rides and access to the model village, model railways and museum.

Detailed Directions by Car:
From All Parts: Devon Railway Centre is situated adjacent to the famous Bickleigh Bridge, just off the A396 Exeter to Tiverton road (3 miles from Tiverton and 8 miles from Exeter).

EASTLEIGH LAKESIDE STEAM RAILWAY

Address: Lakeside Country Park,
Wide Lane, Eastleigh, Hants. SO50 5PE
Telephone Nº: (023) 8061-2020
Year Formed: 1992
Location: Opposite Southampton airport
Length of Line: 1¼ miles

Nº of Steam Locos: 17
Nº of Other Locos: 3
Nº of Members: –
Approx Nº of Visitors P.A.: 60,000
Gauge: 10¼ inches and 7¼ inches
Web site: www.steamtrain.co.uk

GENERAL INFORMATION

Nearest Mainline Station: Southampton Airport
(Parkway) (¼ mile)
Nearest Bus Station: Eastleigh (1½ miles)
Car Parking: Free parking available on site
Coach Parking: Free parking available on site
Souvenir Shop(s): Yes
Food & Drinks: Cafe open every day of the year

SPECIAL INFORMATION

The railway also has a playground and picnic area
overlooking the lakes.

OPERATING INFORMATION

Opening Times: Weekends throughout the year and
daily during July, August and September plus all
school holidays. Open 10.30am to 4.15pm.
Santa Specials run on some dates in December.
Steam Working: As above
Prices: Adult Return £2.50 (First Class £3.00)
Child Return £2.00 (First Class £2.50)
Tickets are available offering 3 return journeys at
reduced rates. Annual season tickets are available.
Children under the age of 2 years ride free of charge.

Detailed Directions by Car:
From All Parts: Exit the M27 at Junction 5 and take the A335 to Eastleigh. The Railway is situated ¼ mile past
Southampton Airport Station on the left hand side of the A335.

EVESHAM VALE LIGHT RAILWAY

Address: Evesham Country Park, Twyford, Evesham WR11 4TP	**Nº of Steam Locos**: 5
Telephone Nº: (01386) 422282	**Nº of Other Locos**: 4
Year Formed: 2002	**Approx Nº of Visitors P.A.**: 50,000
Location of Line: 1 mile north of Evesham	**Gauge**: 15 inches
Length of Line: 1¼ miles	**Web site**: www.evlr.co.uk

GENERAL INFORMATION

Nearest Mainline Station: Evesham (1 mile)
Nearest Bus Station: Evesham (1½ miles)
Car Parking: Available in the Country Park
Coach Parking: Available in the Country Park
Souvenir Shop(s): Yes
Food & Drinks: Restaurant at the Garden Centre

SPECIAL INFORMATION

The railway is situated within the 130 acre Evesham Country Park which has apple orchards and picnic areas overlooking the picturesque Vale of Evesham.

OPERATING INFORMATION

Opening Times: Open at weekends throughout the year and daily during school holidays. Trains run from 10.30am to 5.00pm (until 4.00pm during the winter). Please phone for further details.
Steam Working: Daily when trains are running
Prices: Adult Return £2.00
Child Return £1.40
Senior Citizen Return £1.70

Detailed Directions by Car:
From the North: Exit the M42 at Junction 3 and take the A435 towards Alcester then the A46 to Evesham; From the South: Exit the M5 at Junction 9 and take the A46 to Evesham; From the West: Exit the M5 at Junction 7 and take the A44 to Evesham; From the East: Take the A44 from Oxford to Evesham. Upon reaching Evesham, follow the Brown tourist signs for Evesham Country Park and the railway.

EXBURY GARDENS RAILWAY

Address: Exbury Gardens, Exbury, Near Southampton SO45 1AZ
Telephone N⁰: (02380) 891203
Year Formed: 2001
Location of Line: Exbury
Length of Line: 1½ miles

N⁰ of Steam Locos: 2 at present (a third is scheduled to arrive during May 2008)
N⁰ of Other Locos: 1
N⁰ of Members: None
Approx N⁰ of Visitors P.A.: 55,000
Gauge: 12¼ inches
Web site: www.exbury.co.uk

GENERAL INFORMATION

Nearest Mainline Station: Brockenhurst (8 miles)
Nearest Bus Station: Southampton (12 miles)
Car Parking: Free parking available on site
Coach Parking: Free parking available on site
Souvenir Shop(s): Yes
Food & Drinks: Available

SPECIAL INFORMATION

The railway is located in the world famous Rothschild Azalea and Rhododendron gardens at Exbury in the New Forest. Footplate Experience days are available and the Engine Shed is licensed to host Civil Weddings!

OPERATING INFORMATION

Opening Times: Daily from the 8th March to 9th November. Also open for Santa Specials on 6th, 7th, 13th, 14th, 20th, 21st & 22nd December. Open from 10.00am to 5.30pm (or dusk if earlier)
Steam Working: Every running day from 11.00am.
Prices: Adult Return £3.00
  Child Return £3.00
Note: Day Rover tickets are available during the low season for an additional £1.50 charge.

Detailed Directions by Car:
From all directions: Exit the M27 at Junction 2 and take the A326 to Dibden. Follow the brown tourist signs for Exbury Gardens & Steam Railway.

FAIRBOURNE RAILWAY

Address: Beach Road, Fairbourne, Dolgellau, Gwynedd LL38 2EX	**Nº of Steam Locos**: 4
Telephone Nº: (01341) 250362	**Nº of Other Locos**: 2
Year Formed: 1947	**Nº of Members**: 87
Location of Line: On A493 between Tywyn & Dolgellau	**Annual Membership Fee**: £15.00
	Approx Nº of Visitors P.A.: 18,000
Length of Line: 2 miles	**Gauge**: 12¼ inches
	Web Site: www.fairbournerailway.com

GENERAL INFORMATION

Nearest Mainline Station: Fairbourne (adjacent)
Nearest Bus Station: Fairbourne (adjacent)
Car Parking: Available in Mainline station car park
Coach Parking: Pay & Display car park 300 yards (the Railway will re-imburse car parking charges for party bookings)
Souvenir Shop(s): Yes
Food & Drinks: Yes – Tea room at Fairbourne, Cafe at Barmouth Ferry Terminus

SPECIAL INFORMATION

There is a connecting ferry service (passenger only) to Barmouth from Barmouth Ferry Terminus.

OPERATING INFORMATION

Opening Times: Open over Easter week and during weekends in April. Daily from 3rd May to 21st September (closed on Fridays except from mid-July to the end of August). Also open weekends in October then 27th October to 2nd November. Santa Specials run on 13th and 14th December at 11.30am and 1.30pm.
Steam Working: 11.00am to 3.30pm for normal service. At peak times 10.40am to 4.20pm.
Prices: Adult Return £7.20
Child Return £4.00
Family £18.00 (2 adults + up to 3 children)
Senior Citizen Return £5.80

Detailed Directions by Car:
From North & East Wales: Follow Dolgellau signs, turn left onto A493 towards Tywyn. The turn-off for Fairbourne is located 9 miles south west of Dolgellau; From South Wales: Follow signs for Machynlleth, then follow A487 towards Dolgellau. Then take A493 towards Fairbourne.

FAVERSHAM MINIATURE RAILWAY

Address: Brogdale Farm, Brogdale Road, Faversham, Kent **Telephone Nº**: (01795) 537919 **Year Formed**: 1984 **Location of Line**: Faversham, Kent **Length of Line**: ½ mile at present **Gauge**: 9 inches	**Nº of Steam Locos**: 2 **Nº of Other Locos**: 9 **Nº of Members**: 40 **Annual Membership Fee**: £10.00 Adult, £25.00 Family **Approx Nº of Visitors P.A.**: 3,500 **Web site**: www.fmrs.org.uk

GENERAL INFORMATION

Nearest Mainline Station: Faversham (¾ mile)
Nearest Bus Station: None, but a regular bus service travels to Faversham from Canterbury
Car Parking: Available on site
Coach Parking: Available on site
Souvenir Shop(s): Various shops on site
Food & Drinks: Available

SPECIAL INFORMATION

Faversham Miniature Railway is the only 9 inch gauge railway open to the public in the UK.

OPERATING INFORMATION

Opening Times: Sundays and Bank Holiday weekends from March to November.
Steam Working: Special steam days only. Please contact the Railway for further details.
Prices: £1.00 per ride

Detailed Directions by Car:
Exit the M2 at Junction 5 and take the A251 towards Faversham. After about ½ mile turn left onto the A2 then left again after ¼ mile turning into Brogdale Road for the Farm and Railway.

FERRY MEADOWS MINIATURE RAILWAY

Address: Ham Lane, Nene Park,
Oundle Road, Peterborough   PE2 5UU
Telephone Nº: (01933) 398889
Year Formed: 1978
Location of Line: Nene Leisure Park
Length of Line: 700 yards

Nº of Steam Locos: 1
Nº of Other Locos: 1
Approx Nº of Visitors P.A.: Not known
Gauge: 10¼ inches
Web site: www.ferrymeadowsrailway.co.uk

GENERAL INFORMATION

Nearest Mainline Station: Peterborough (2 miles)
Nearest Bus Station: Peterborough (2 miles)
Car Parking: Available adjacent
Coach Parking: Available adjacent
Souvenir Shop(s): Yes
Food & Drinks: Available

SPECIAL INFORMATION

The railway is situated in the Ferry Meadows area of
Nene Park in which watersports and other leisure
activities are also available.

OPERATING INFORMATION

Opening Times: Every weekend from 1st March to
2nd November 2008 and daily during the school
holidays (though closed on Mondays). Trains run
from 11.00am to 4.50pm.

Steam Working: Bank Holidays and weekends in
August.

Prices: Adult Return £2.50
              Child Return £1.50

Detailed Directions by Car:
Nene Park is situated on the A605 Oundle Road. Follow the brown tourist signs for Nene Valley Park.

FFESTINIOG RAILWAY

Address: Ffestiniog Railway, Harbour Station, Porthmadog, Gwynedd LL49 9NF **Telephone Nº**: (01766) 516000 **Year Formed**: 1832 **Location of Line**: Porthmadog to Blaenau Ffestiniog **Length of Line**: 13½ miles	**Nº of Steam Locos**: 12 **Nº of Other Locos**: 12 **Nº of Members**: 5,000 **Annual Membership Fee**: £22.00 **Approx Nº of Visitors P.A.**: 140,000 **Gauge**: 1 foot 11½ inches **Web Site**: www.festrail.co.uk

GENERAL INFORMATION

Nearest Mainline Station: Blaenau Ffestiniog (interchange) or Minffordd
Nearest Bus Station: Bus stop next to stations at Porthmadog & Blaenau Ffestiniog
Car Parking: Parking available at Porthmadog, Blaenau Ffestiniog and Minffordd
Coach Parking: Available at Porthmadog and Blaenau Ffestiniog
Souvenir Shop(s): Yes
Food & Drinks: Yes

SPECIAL INFORMATION

The Railway runs through the spectacular scenery of Snowdonia National Park.

OPERATING INFORMATION

Opening Times: Daily service from the 15th March to 2nd November. Also a number of other dates during March and a limited service in the Winter. Train times vary. Contact the railway for details.
Steam Working: Most trains are steam hauled. Limited in the Winter, however.
Prices: Adult £17.50 (All-day Rover ticket)
One child travels free with each adult, additional children travel for half the fare.
Reductions are available for Senior Citizens, Families and groups of 20 or more. Single fares are cheaper than Day Rover tickets.

Detailed Directions by Car:
Portmadog is easily accessible from the Midlands – take the M54/A5 to Corwen then the A494 to Bala onto the A4212 to Trawsfynydd and the A470 (becomes the A487 from Maentwrog) to Porthmadog. From Chester take the A55 to Llandudno Junction and the A470 to Blaenau Ffestiniog. Both Stations are well-signposted.

GARTELL LIGHT RAILWAY

Address: Common Lane, Yenston, Templecombe, Somerset   BA8 0NB
Telephone Nº: (01963) 370752
Year Formed: 1991
Location of Line: South of Templecombe
Length of Line: ¾ mile

Nº of Steam Locos: 1
Nº of Other Locos: 3
Approx Nº of Visitors P.A.: 3,000
Gauge: 2 feet
Web site: www.glr-online.co.uk

GENERAL INFORMATION

Nearest Mainline Station: Templecombe (1¼ miles)
Nearest Bus Station: Wincanton
Car Parking: Free parking adjacent to the station
Coach Parking: Adjacent to the station
Souvenir Shop(s): Yes
Food & Drinks: Meals, snacks and drinks available

SPECIAL INFORMATION

The railway is fully signalled using a variety of semaphore, colour-light and shunting signals, controlled by signalmen in two operational signal boxes. Part of the line runs along the track bed of the old Somerset & Dorset Joint Railway.

OPERATING INFORMATION

Opening Times: 2008 dates: 24th March; 5th May, 26th May; 29th June; 27th July; 3rd, 10th, 17th, 24th, 25th & 31st August; 28th September and 26th October. Trains depart at frequent intervals between 10.30am and 4.30pm
Steam Working: Every day the railway is operating
Prices: Adult £6.00
　　　　　　Senior Citizen £4.50
　　　　　　Child £3.00
Note: Tickets permit unlimited travel by any train on the day of purchase. Under-5s travel for free.

Detailed Directions by Car:
From All Parts: The Railway is situated off the A357 just south of Templecombe and on open days is clearly indicated by the usual brown tourist signs.

GIANT'S CAUSEWAY & BUSHMILLS RAILWAY

Address: Giant's Causeway Station, Runkerry Road, Bushmills, Co. Antrim, Northern Ireland BT57 8SZ **Telephone Nº**: (028) 2073-2844 **Information Line**: (028) 2073-2594 **Year Formed**: 2002 **Location**: Between the distillery village of Bushmills and the Giant's Causeway	**Length of Line**: 2 miles **Nº of Steam Locos**: 2 **Nº of Other Locos**: 1 **Nº of Members**: None **Approx Nº of Visitors P.A.**: 50,000 **Gauge**: 3 feet **Web site**: www.freewebs.com/giantscausewayrailway

GENERAL INFORMATION

Nearest Northern Ireland Railway Station: Coleraine/Portrush

Nearest Bus Station: Coleraine/Portrush

Car Parking: Car Park fee at Giant's Causeway Station is refunded upon ticket purchase. By parking at the Bushmills Station and taking the railway expensive parking charges at the Causeway itself can be avoided.

Coach Parking: Available on site

Souvenir Shop(s): Yes

Food & Drinks: At Giant's Causeway Station only

SPECIAL INFORMATION

The railway links the distillery village of Bushmills (open to visitors) to the World Heritage Site of the Giant's Causeway. The railway itself is built on the final two miles of the pioneering hydro-electric tramway which linked the Giant's Causeway to the main railway at Portrush from 1883 to 1949.

OPERATING INFORMATION

Opening Times: Daily in July and August, over St. Patrick's Day weekend and for Easter week. Also open at weekends from Easter to the end of June and in October & September. Trains run from 11.00am.

Steam Working: Usually daily. Please ring the Information Line shown above for more details.

Prices: Adult Return £6.75
Adult Single £5.25
Child Return £4.25
Child Single £3.25

Note: Family Tickets and group rates are available.

Detailed Directions by Car:

From Belfast take the M2 to the junction with the A26 (for Antrim, Ballymena and Coleraine). Follow the A26/M2/A26. From Ballymoney onwards Bushmills and the Giant's Causeway are well signposted. The railway is also well signposted in the immediate vicinity.

GOLDEN VALLEY LIGHT RAILWAY

Address: Butterley Station, Ripley, Derbyshire DE5 3QZ
Telephone Nº: (01773) 747674
Year Formed: 1987
Location of Line: Butterley, near Ripley
Length of Line: Four-fifths of a mile
Web site: www.gvlr.org.uk

Nº of Steam Locos: 2
Nº of Other Locos: 23
Nº of Members: 75
Annual Membership Fee: £16.00
Approx Nº of Visitors P.A.: 10,000
Gauge: 2 feet

GENERAL INFORMATION

Nearest Mainline Station: Alfreton (6 miles)
Nearest Bus Station: Bus stop outside the Station
Car Parking: Free parking at site – ample space
Coach Parking: Free parking at site
Souvenir Shop(s): Yes – at Butterley and Swanwick
Food & Drinks: Yes – both sites

SPECIAL INFORMATION

The Golden Valley Light Railway is part of the Midland Railway – Butterley and runs from the museum site through the country park to Newlands Inn Station close to the Cromford Canal and the pub of the same name.

OPERATING INFORMATION

Opening Times: Weekends and Bank Holidays from April to October and daily from 21st to 25th March, 26th May to 1st June and 23rd July to 1st September. Trains run from 11.45pm onwards.
Steam Working: One weekend per month – please contact the railway for further details. There is also a Gala Weekend with visiting locos scheduled on 12th and 13th July 2008.
Prices: Adult £2.00
 Children £1.00

Detailed Directions by Car:
From All Parts: From the M1 exit at Junction 28 and take the A38 towards Derby. The Centre is signposted at the junction with the B6179.

GREAT WHIPSNADE RAILWAY

Address: ZSL Whipsnade Zoo, Dunstable LU6 2LF **Telephone N°**: (01582) 872171 **Year Formed**: 1970 **Location of Line**: ZSL Whipsnade Zoo, Near Dunstable **Length of Line**: 1¾ miles	**N° of Steam Locos**: 2 **N° of Other Locos**: 5 **N° of Members**: None **Approx N° of Visitors P.A.**: 130,000 **Gauge**: 2 feet 6 inches **Web site**: www.zsl.org

GENERAL INFORMATION

Nearest Mainline Station: Luton (7 miles)
Nearest Bus Station: Dunstable (3 miles)
Car Parking: Available just outside the park
Coach Parking: Available just outside the park
Souvenir Shop(s): Next to the Station
Food & Drinks: Available

SPECIAL INFORMATION

The Railway is situated in the ZSL Whipsnade Zoo operated by the Zoological Society of London.

OPERATING INFORMATION

Opening Times: The zoo is open daily from 10.00am throughout the year. Closing time varies from 4.00pm to 6.00pm depending on the time of the year. The railway runs daily from 31st March until 28th October and at weekends at some other times of the year. Contact the zoo for further details.
Steam Working: Every operating day.
Prices: Adult £12.00
         Child £9.00
         Family Ticket £37.50
         Senior Citizen £10.50
Note: The above prices are for entrance into the Zoo itself. Train rides are an additional charge for adult but free for children.

Detailed Directions by Car:
From All Parts: Exit the M1 at Junction 11 and take the A505 then the B489. Follow signs for Whipsnade Zoo.

GROUDLE GLEN RAILWAY

Address: Groudle Glen, Onchan, Isle of Man	**Nº of Steam Locos**: 2
Telephone Nº: (01624) 670453 (weekends)	**Nº of Other Locos**: 2
Year Formed: 1982 **Re-Opened**: 1986	**Nº of Members**: 600
Location of Line: Groudle Glen	**Annual Membership Fee**: £10.00
Length of Line: ¾ mile	**Approx Nº of Visitors P.A.**: 10,000
Gauge: 2 feet	**Correspondence**: 29 Hawarden Avenue, Douglas, Isle of Man IM1 4BP
	Web site: www.groudleglenrailway.com

GENERAL INFORMATION

Nearest Mainline Station: Manx Electric Railway
Nearest Bus Station: Douglas Bus Station
Car Parking: At the entrance to the Glen
Coach Parking: At the entrance to the Glen
Souvenir Shop(s): Yes
Food & Drinks: Coffee and Tea available

SPECIAL INFORMATION

The Railway runs through a picturesque glen to a coastal headland where there are the remains of a Victorian Zoo. The Railway was built in 1896 and closed in 1962.

OPERATING INFORMATION

Opening Times: Easter Sunday & Monday + Sundays from 4th May to 28th September 11.00am to 4.30pm. Also Tuesday evenings from 29th July to 19th August and Wednesday evenings from 2nd July to 20th August – 7.00pm to 9.00pm. Santa trains run on 14th, 20th and 21st December + Boxing Day. An Enthusiasts Weekend is scheduled on 19th and 20th July from 11.00am to 4.30pm.
Steam Working: Phone the Railway for details.
Prices: Adult Return £3.00
        Child Return £1.50
        Santa train fares £5.00

Detailed Directions by Car:
The Railway is situated on the coast road to the north of Douglas.

Hall Leys Miniature Railway

Address: Hall Leys Park, Matlock, Derbyshire
Telephone Nº: 07734 449359
Year Formed: 1948
Location of Line: Hall Leys Park
Length of Line: 200 yards

Nº of Steam Locos: None
Nº of Other Locos: 1
Approx Nº of Visitors P.A.: Not known
Gauge: 9½ inches

GENERAL INFORMATION

Nearest Mainline Station: Matlock (½ mile)
Nearest Bus Station: Matlock (by the train station)
Car Parking: Available near the train station on the new bypass
Coach Parking: As above

SPECIAL INFORMATION

The Hall Leys Miniature Railway has operated in Matlock since 1948 and is one of only 4 railways in the country to run a line with the unusual 9½ inch gauge.

OPERATING INFORMATION

Opening Times: Weekends from Easter to September and daily on the school holidays during this period.
Steam Working: None at present.
Prices: 60p per ride.

Detailed Directions by Car:
Hall Leys Park is situated in the centre of Matlock between the River Derwent and the A615 Causeway Lane.

HAYLING SEASIDE RAILWAY

Address: Beachlands, Sea Front Road, Hayling Island, Hampshire   PO11 9AG
Telephone Nº: (02392) 372427
Year Formed: 2001
Location: Beachlands to Eastoke Corner
Length of Line: 1 mile
Web site: www.easthaylinglightrailway.co.uk

Nº of Steam Locos: Visiting locos only
Nº of Other Locos: 4
Nº of Members: Approximately 100
Annual Membership Fee: £10.00
Approx Nº of Visitors P.A.: 25,000
Gauge: 2 feet

GENERAL INFORMATION

Nearest Mainline Station: Havant
Nearest Bus Station: Beachlands
Car Parking: Spaces are available at both Beachlands and Eastoke Corner.
Coach Parking: Beachlands and Eastoke Corner
Souvenir Shop(s): Yes
Food & Drinks: Available

SPECIAL INFORMATION

The Railway runs along Hayling Island beach front where there are fantastic views across the Solent to the Isle of Wight.

OPERATING INFORMATION

Opening Times: Every Saturday, Sunday and Wednesday throughout the year and daily during the School holidays. Various specials run at different times of the year – please check the web site or phone the Railway for further details. The first train normally departs at 11.00am from Beachlands.
Steam Working: Visiting locos only. Please contact the railway for further information.
Prices: Adult Return £3.50
       Child/Senior Citizen Return £2.00
       Family Return £7.00 (2 Adult + 2 Child)
       Dogs travel free of charge!

Detailed Directions by Car:
Exit the A27 at Havant Roundabout and proceed to Hayling Island and Beachlands Station following the road signs. Parking is available south of the Carousel Amusement Park. Beachlands Station is within the car park.

HEATHERSLAW LIGHT RAILWAY

Address: Ford Forge, Heatherslaw, Cornhill-on-Tweed TD12 4TJ	**N° of Steam Locos**: 1
Telephone N°: (01890) 820244	**N° of Other Locos**: 1
Year Formed: 1989	**N° of Members**: None
Location of Line: Ford & Etal Estates between Wooler & Berwick	**Approx N° of Visitors P.A.**: 30,000
	Gauge: 15 inches
	Web site: www.ford-and-etal.co.uk
Length of Line: 2 miles	or www.secretkingdom.com

GENERAL INFORMATION

Nearest Mainline Station: Berwick-upon-Tweed (10 miles)
Nearest Bus Station: Berwick-upon-Tweed (10 mls)
Car Parking: Available on site
Coach Parking: Available on site
Souvenir Shop(s): Yes
Food & Drinks: Available

SPECIAL INFORMATION

The Railway follows the River Till from Heatherslaw to Etal Village. All coaching stock is built on site.

OPERATING INFORMATION

Opening Times: Daily from 17th March to 2nd November 2008. Trains run hourly between 11.00am and 3.00pm
Steam Working: Daily except when maintenance is is being carried out on the engine.
Prices: Adult Return £6.00
            Child Return £4.00   (Under 5's: £1.00)
            Senior Citizen Return £5.00

Detailed Directions by Car:
From the North: Take the A697 from Coldstream and the railway is about 5 miles along.
From the South: Take the A697 from Wooler and Millfield.

HOLLYCOMBE STEAM COLLECTION

Address: Hollycombe, Liphook, Hants. GU30 7LP
Telephone Nº: (01428) 724900
Year Formed: 1970
Location of Line: Hollycombe, Liphook
Length of Line: 1¾ miles Narrow gauge, ¼ mile Standard gauge

Nº of Steam Locos: 6
Nº of Other Locos: 2
Nº of Members: 100
Annual Membership Fee: £8.00
Approx Nº of Visitors P.A.: 35,000
Gauge: 2 feet plus Standard & 7¼ inches
Web site: www.hollycombe.co.uk

GENERAL INFORMATION

Nearest Mainline Station: Liphook (1 mile)
Nearest Bus Station: Liphook
Car Parking: Extensive grass area
Coach Parking: Hardstanding
Souvenir Shop(s): Yes
Food & Drinks: Yes – Cafe

SPECIAL INFORMATION

The narrow gauge railway ascends to spectacular views of the Downs and is part of an extensive working steam museum.

OPERATING INFORMATION

Opening Times: Sundays and Bank Holidays from Easter until the first week in October. Open daily from 29th July to 27th August 2008.
Steam Working: 1.00pm to 5.00pm
Prices: Adult £11.00
 Child £9.00
 Senior Citizen £10.00
 Family £38.00 (2 adults + 3 children)
Note: Prices may vary throughout the year. Please contact the Railway for further details.

Detailed Directions by Car:
Take the A3 to Liphook and follow the brown tourist signs for the railway.

HYTHE FERRY PIER RAILWAY

Address: Hythe Ferry Pier, Prospect Place, Hythe SO45 6AU **Telephone N°**: (023) 8084-0722 **Year Formed**: Installed 1921 **Location of Line**: Hythe Pier **Length of Line**: 600 metres	**N° of Steam Locos**: None **N° of Other Locos**: 2 **N° of Members**: – **Approx N° of Visitors P.A.**: 500,000 **Gauge**: 2 feet **Web site**: www.hytheferry.co.uk

GENERAL INFORMATION

Nearest Mainline Station: Southampton (2 miles)
Nearest Bus Station: Southampton (2 miles)
Car Parking: Paid parking nearby
Coach Parking: Paid parking nearby
Souvenir Shop(s): Yes
Food & Drinks: Yes

SPECIAL INFORMATION

The railway operates along a Victorian Pier and takes passengers to a ferry which operates a regular half-hourly service crossing the harbour from Hythe to Southampton. This is the world's oldest continually working pier train.

OPERATING INFORMATION

Opening Times: The ferry and therefore railway operates daily. The first ferry departs Hythe at 6.10am on weekdays and 7.10am on Saturdays. Sundays and Bank Holidays run from 9.40am to 6.00pm.
Prices: Pier Entrance fee 90p (included in the cost of a Ferry ticket)
Note: Ferry fares are an additional charge and vary depending whether they are peak or off-peak.

Detailed Directions by Car:
Hythe Ferry Pier is located by the waterside in Hythe adjacent to the Promenade and the Marina.

ISLE OF MAN STEAM RAILWAY

Address: Isle of Man Railways, Banks Circus, Douglas, Isle of Man IM1 5PT	**Nº of Steam Locos**: 7
Telephone Nº: (01624) 663366	**Nº of Other Locos**: 2
Year Formed: 1873	**Nº of Members**: –
Location of Line: Douglas to Port Erin	**Annual Membership Fee**: –
Length of Line: 15½ miles	**Approx Nº of Visitors P.A.**: 140,000
	Gauge: 3 feet

GENERAL INFORMATION

Nearest Mainline Station: Not applicable
Car Parking: Limited parking at all stations
Coach Parking: Available at Douglas & Port Erin
Souvenir Shop(s): At Port Erin station
Food & Drinks: Yes – Douglas & Port Erin stations

SPECIAL INFORMATION

The Isle of Man Steam Railway is operated by the Isle of Man Government.

OPERATING INFORMATION

Opening Times: 2008 Dates: Daily from 17th March to 2nd November.
Steam Working: All scheduled services
Prices: Prices vary with 1, 3 & 7 day Explorer tickets also available which include travel on buses, the Snaefell and Manx Electric Railways and Douglas Corporation Horse Trams.

Detailed Directions:
By Sea from Heysham (Lancashire) or Liverpool to reach Isle of Man. By Air from Belfast, Dublin, Glasgow, Liverpool, Manchester, Newcastle, Bristol and London. Douglas Station is ½ mile inland from the Sea terminal at the end of North Quay.

KERR'S MINIATURE RAILWAY

Address: West Links Park, Arbroath, Tayside, Scotland	**Nº of Steam Locos:** 2
Telephone Nº: (01241) 874074 or 879249	**Nº of Other Locos:** 4
Year Formed: 1935	**Nº of Members:** None
Location: Seafront, West Links Park	**Annual Membership Fee:** –
Length of Line: 400 yards	**Approx Nº of Visitors P.A.:** 10,000
Web site: www.kerrsminiaturerailway.co.uk	**Gauge:** 10¼ inches

GENERAL INFORMATION

Nearest Mainline Station: Arbroath (1½ miles)
Nearest Bus Station: Arbroath (1½ miles)
Car Parking: Available 600 yards from railway
Coach Parking: Available 600 yards from railway
Souvenir Shop(s): Gifts on special event days
Food & Drinks: Cafe stall in West Links Park

SPECIAL INFORMATION

The Railway is Scotland's oldest passenger-carrying miniature railway. It is a family-run enterprise not run for profit which is staffed by volunteers. The track itself runs alongside the Dundee to Aberdeen mainline.

OPERATING INFORMATION

Opening Times: Weekends only in April, May, June and September. Daily during July and the first half of August then weekends only for the second half of August. Opening times are 11.00am to 4.00pm.
Steam Working: No set pattern but Steam is more likely to be running on Sundays than other dates.
Prices: All tickets £1.00

Detailed Directions by Car:
From All Parts: West Links Park is a seaside location which runs parallel to the A92 Coastal Tourist Route in Arbroath. Turn off the A92 at the Seaforth Hotel for parking. The railway is then 600 yards due West along the seafront.

KIRKLEES LIGHT RAILWAY

Address: Park Mill Way, Clayton West, near Huddersfield, W. Yorks. HD8 9XJ	**Nº of Steam Locos**: 4
Telephone Nº: (01484) 865727	**Nº of Other Locos**: 2
Year Formed: 1991	**Nº of Members**: –
Location of Line: Clayton West to Shelley	**Approx Nº of Visitors P.A.**: 48,000
Length of Line: 4 miles	**Gauge**: 15 inches
	Web site: www.kirkleeslightrailway.com

GENERAL INFORMATION

Nearest Mainline Station: Denby Dale (4 miles)
Nearest Bus Station: Bus stop outside gates. Take the 435 from Wakefield or the 80 and 81 from Huddersfield/Barnsley.
Car Parking: Ample free parking at site
Coach Parking: Ample free parking at site
Souvenir Shop(s): Yes
Food & Drinks: Yes

SPECIAL INFORMATION

The Railway now has both indoor and outdoor play areas for children, the outdoor area is train themed and is fully compliant with all safety regulations.

OPERATING INFORMATION

Opening Times: Open every weekend and most school holidays in the Winter. Open daily from 19th July to 7th September.
Steam Working: All trains are steam-hauled. Trains run hourly from 11.00am to 4.00pm
Prices: Adults £6.50
Children (3-15 years) £4.50
Children (under 3 years) Free of charge
Concessions £5.50
Family Ticket £20.00
Note: Prices at Special events may vary.

Detailed Directions by Car:
The Railway is located on the A636 Wakefield to Denby Dale road. Turn off the M1 at Junction 39 and follow the A636 signposted for Denby Dale. Continue for approximately 4 miles then the railway is on the left after passing under the railway bridge and is situated at the top of the Industrial Estate, just before the village of Scissett.

KNEBWORTH PARK MINIATURE RAILWAY

Address: c/o Estate Office, Knebworth, Hertfordshire SG3 6PY **Telephone Nº**: (01438) 812661 **Year Formed**: 1991 (Miniature Railway) **Location of Line**: Knebworth Park **Length of Line**: 800 yards	**Nº of Steam Locos**: One **Nº of Other Locos**: 6 **Nº of Members**: None **Approx Nº of Visitors P.A.**: 44,000 **Gauge**: 10¼ inches **Web site**: www.knebworthrailway.co.nr

GENERAL INFORMATION

Nearest Mainline Station: Knebworth
Nearest Bus Station: Stevenage
Car Parking: Available on site
Coach Parking: Available on site
Souvenir Shop(s): Yes
Food & Drinks: Yes

SPECIAL INFORMATION

The Railway is located in the grounds of the historic Knebworth House.

OPERATING INFORMATION

Opening Times: Daily from 21st March to 6th April, 24th May to 1st June and 28th June to 3rd September. Closed on 5th July. Open on weekends and Bank Holidays only from 12th April to 18th May, 7th to 22nd June and 6th to 28th September inclusive. Trains run from 12.00pm to 5.00pm on these dates.
Steam Working: Please contact the railway for further details.
Prices: Adult £7.50 – £9.50
Child/Senior Citizen £7.50–£9.00
Family Ticket £26.00 – £33.00
Note: Prices shown above are for entrance into Knebworth Park and House. One free train ride is included with the entrance fee. Subsequent rides are charged as follows: Adult £1.50   Child £1.20

Detailed Directions by Car:
From All Parts: Exit the A1(M) at Junction 7 and follow signs for Knebworth Park. After entering the Park, follow signs for the Adventure Playground for the Railway.

LAPPA VALLEY STEAM RAILWAY

Address: St. Newlyn East, Newquay, Cornwall TR8 5LX	**Nº of Steam Locos**: 2
Telephone Nº: (01872) 510317	**Nº of Other Locos**: 2
Year Formed: 1974	**Nº of Members**: –
Location of Line: Benny Halt to East Wheal Rose, near St. Newlyn East	**Annual Membership Fee**: –
Length of Line: 1 mile	**Approx Nº of Visitors P.A.**: 50,000
	Gauge: 15 inches
	Web site: www.lappavalley.co.uk

GENERAL INFORMATION

Nearest Mainline Station: Newquay (5 miles)
Nearest Bus Station: Newquay (5 miles)
Car Parking: Free parking at Benny Halt
Coach Parking: Free parking at Benny Halt
Souvenir Shop(s): Yes
Food & Drinks: Yes

SPECIAL INFORMATION

The railway runs on part of the former Newquay to Chacewater branch line. Site also has a Grade II listed mine building, boating, play areas for children and 2 other miniature train rides.

OPERATING INFORMATION

Opening Times: Easter to October (daily to 30th September). Limited opening during October – please phone the Railway for further details.
Steam Working: 10.30am to 4.30pm or later on operating days
Prices: Adult £9.20 (Off-peak £6.80
Child/Senior Citizen £7.50
(Off-peak £5.20)
Family £29.50 (Off-peak £21.50)
(2 adults + 2 children)

Detailed Directions by Car:
The railway is signposted from the A30 at the Summercourt-Mitchell bypass, from the A3075 south of Newquay and the A3058 east of Newquay.

LAUNCESTON STEAM RAILWAY

Address: The Old Gasworks, St. Thomas Road, Launceston, Cornwall   PL15 8DA
Telephone Nº: (01566) 775665
Year Formed: Opened in 1983
Location of Line: Launceston to Newmills
Length of Line: 2½ miles

Nº of Steam Locos: 5 (3 working)
Nº of Other Locos: 2 Diesel, 2 Electric
Nº of Members: Not applicable
Annual Membership Fee: –
Gauge: 1 foot 11 $^5/_8$ inches
Web site: www.launcestonsr.co.uk

GENERAL INFORMATION

Nearest Mainline Station: Liskeard (15 miles)
Nearest Bus Station: Launceston (½ mile)
Car Parking: At Station, Newport Industrial Estate, Launceston
Coach Parking: As above
Souvenir Shop(s): Yes – also with a bookshop
Food & Drinks: Yes – Cafe, snacks & drinks

SPECIAL INFORMATION

During the Summer school holidays, two engines are sometimes in operation. The 25th Anniversary of the opening of the railway is celebrated in 2008.

OPERATING INFORMATION

Opening Times: Daily during Easter Week and from 25th May until the 21st September but closed on Saturdays.
Steam Working: 11.00am to 4.50pm.
Prices: Adult £8.25
            Child £5.50
            Family £25.00 (2 adults + 4 children)
            Senior Citizen £6.50
Group rates are available upon application. These prices include as many trips as you like on the day of purchase.

Detailed Directions by Car:
From the East/West: Drive to Launceston via the A30 and look for the brown Steam Engine Tourist signs. Use the L.S.R. car park at the Newport Industrial Estate; From Bude/Holsworthy: Take the A388 to Launceston and follow signs for the town centre. After the river bridge turn left at the traffic lights into Newport Industrial Estate and use the L.S.R. car park.

LEADHILLS & WANLOCKHEAD RAILWAY

Address: The Station, Leadhills, Lanarkshire   ML12 6XS
Telephone Nº: None
Year Formed: 1983
Location of Line: Leadhills, Lanarkshire
Length of Line: ¾ mile (at present)

Nº of Steam Locos: None at present
Nº of Other Locos: 4
Nº of Members: Approximately 100
Annual Membership Fee: Adult £8.00
Approx Nº of Visitors P.A.: 2,500
Gauge: 2 feet
Web site: www.leadhillsrailway.co.uk

GENERAL INFORMATION

Nearest Mainline Station: Sanquhar
Nearest Bus Station: Lanark and Sanquhar
Car Parking: Available on site
Coach Parking: Available on site
Souvenir Shop(s): Yes
Food & Drinks: Yes

SPECIAL INFORMATION

Leadhills & Wanlockhead Railway is the highest adhesion railway in the UK with the summit 1,498 feet above sea level.

OPERATING INFORMATION

Opening Times: Weekends and Bank Holidays from Easter until the end of October (Sundays only in October). Trains run from 11.20am to 4.20pm
Steam Working: None at present
Prices: Adult Day Ticket £3.00
　　　　　　 Child Day Ticket £1.00
　　　　　　 Family Day Ticket £7.00
　　　　　　　　(2 adults and up to 6 children)
　　　　　　 Senior Citizen Day Ticket £2.50

Detailed Directions by Car:
From the South: Exit the M74 at Junction 14 and follow the A702 to Elvanfoot. Turn right onto the B7040 and follow to Leadhills. Turn left at the T-junction and Station Road is a short distance on the left; From the North: Exit the M74 at Junction 13 for Abington and follow signs for Leadhills along the B797. Station Road is on the left shortly after entering Leadhills.

LEIGHTON BUZZARD RAILWAY

Address: Pages Park Station, Billington Road, Leighton Buzzard, Beds. LU7 4TN	**N⁰ of Steam Locos**: 12
	N⁰ of Other Locos: 41
Telephone N⁰: (01525) 373888	**N⁰ of Members**: 400
Year Formed: 1967	**Annual Membership Fee**: £18.00
Location of Line: Leighton Buzzard	**Approx N⁰ of Visitors P.A.**: 21,000
Length of Line: 3 miles	**Gauge**: 2 feet
	Web site: www.buzzrail.co.uk

GENERAL INFORMATION

Nearest Mainline Station: Leighton Buzzard (2 miles)
Nearest Bus Station: Leighton Buzzard (¾ mile)
Car Parking: Free parking adjacent
Coach Parking: Free parking adjacent
Souvenir Shop(s): Yes
Food & Drinks: Yes

OPERATING INFORMATION

Opening Times: Sundays from 16th March to 26th October plus Bank Holiday weekends. Also open on some Saturdays and weekdays. Trains run from mid-morning to late afternoon and Santa Specials run on some dates in December. Please contact the railway or visit the web site for further details.
Steam Working: Most operating days.
Prices: Adult £7.00
　　　　　 Child £3.00
　　　　　 Senior Citizens £6.00
　　　　　 Family Ticket £19.00 (2 Adult + 2 Child)
　　　　　 Family Ticket £16.00 (2 Adult + 1 Child)

Detailed Directions by Car:
Follow the brown tourist signs in Leighton Buzzard. Pages Park Station is ¾ mile from the Town Centre on the Hemel Hempstead road. From the A505/A4146 bypass, turn towards Leighton Buzzard Town Centre at the McDonalds roundabout, following 'Narrow Gauge Railway' signs.

LLANBERIS LAKE RAILWAY

Address: Gilfach Ddu, Llanberis, Gwynedd LL55 4TY	**Nº of Steam Locos**: 3
Telephone Nº: (01286) 870549	**Nº of Other Locos**: 4
Year Formed: 1970	**Nº of Members**: –
Location of Line: Just off the A4086	**Annual Membership Fee**: –
Caernarfon to Capel Curig road at Llanberis	**Approx Nº of Visitors P.A.**: 70,000
Length of Line: 2½ miles	**Gauge**: 1 foot 11½ inches
	Web site: www.lake-railway.co.uk

GENERAL INFORMATION

Nearest Mainline Station: Bangor (8 miles)
Nearest Bus Station: Caernarfon (6 miles)
Car Parking: £3.00 Council car park on site
Coach Parking: Ample free parking on site
Souvenir Shop(s): Yes
Food & Drinks: Yes

SPECIAL INFORMATION

Llanberis Lake Railway runs along part of the trackbed of the Padarn Railway which transported slates for export and closed in 1961. An extension to Llanberis village opened in June 2003.

OPERATING INFORMATION

Opening Times: Open most days from mid-March to 31st October, daily from June to August and on certain days during the winter. Please send for a free timetable or check out the railway's web site.
Steam Working: Every operating day. Trains generally run from 11.00am to 4.00pm.
Prices: Adult £6.50
Child £4.50
Family ticket £19.00 (2 Adult + 2 Children)
A range of other family discounts are also available.
Note: The Welsh Slate Museum is adjacent to the Railway.

Detailed Directions by Car:
The railway is situated just off the A4086 Caernarfon to Capel Curig road. Follow signs for Padarn Country Park.

LYNTON & BARNSTAPLE RAILWAY

Address: Woody Bay Station, Martinhoe Cross, Parracombe, Devon   EX31 4RA
Telephone Nº: (01598) 763487
Year Formed: 1993
Location of Line: North Devon
Length of Line: One mile

Nº of Steam Locos: 2
Nº of Other Locos: 4
Nº of Members: 2,200
Annual Membership Fee: £18.00
Approx Nº of Visitors P.A.: 40,000
Gauge: 1 foot 11½ inches
Web site: www.lynton-rail.co.uk

GENERAL INFORMATION

Nearest Mainline Station: Barnstaple
Nearest Bus Station: Barnstaple
Car Parking: Available at Woody Bay Station
Coach Parking: Available by prior arrangement
Souvenir Shop(s): Yes – at Woody Bay Station
Food & Drinks: Available at Woody Bay Station

SPECIAL INFORMATION

Passengers were first carried on a short stretch of this scenic narrow-gauge railway in July 2004. This was the first time the track had been used since the original railway closed in September 1935. The ultimate aim of the Lynton & Barnstaple Railway Trust is to re-open all 19 miles of the line.

OPERATING INFORMATION

Opening Times: Open most days from Easter until the end of October and selected dates in November and December. Please check with the railway for exact dates. Trains run from 11.00am to 4.00pm.
Steam Working: All trains are steam-hauled except in the event of breakdown, failure or other obstruction of service.
Prices: Adult Return £5.00
        Child Return £3.00 (Under-14s)
        Senior Citizen Return £4.00
        Family Ticket £13 (2 Adult + 3 Children)

Detailed Directions by Car:
From All Parts: Woody Bay Station is located alongside the A39 halfway between Lynton and Blackmoor Gate and one mile north-east of the village of Parracombe.

MARKEATON PARK LIGHT RAILWAY

Address: Markeaton Park, Derby, DE22	**Nº of Steam Locos**: 1
Telephone Nº: (01623) 552292	**Nº of Other Locos**: 1
Year Formed: 1989	**Approx Nº of Visitors P.A.**: Not known
Location of Line: Markeaton Park	**Gauge**: 15 inches
Length of Line: 1,400 yards	
Web site: www.markeaton-lady.derby-in-derbyshire.org.uk	

GENERAL INFORMATION

Nearest Mainline Station: Derby (2 miles)
Nearest Bus Station: Derby (2 miles)
Car Parking: Available adjacent to the railway
Coach Parking: Available
Souvenir Shop(s): Yes
Food & Drinks: Available

SPECIAL INFORMATION

Markeaton Park Light Railway opened in 1996 and now runs from the main car park, over two major bridges to a second terminus adjacent to the play area at Mundy Halt.

OPERATING INFORMATION

Opening Times: During weekends and school holidays throughout the year with trains running hourly from 11.00am to 4.00pm.
Steam Working: Most services are steam hauled.
Prices: Single £1.00   Return £2.00

Detailed Directions by Car:
Markeaton Park is situated in the North-West corner of Derby just to the North of the Junction between the A38 Queensway and A52 Ashbourne Road. The railway itself is situated adjacent to the main car park.

MULL & WEST HIGHLAND RAILWAY

Address: Old Pier Station, Craignure,
Isle of Mull, Argyll PA65 6AY
Telephone Nº: (01680) 812494/812567
Web site: www.mullrail.co.uk
Year Formed: 1983
Location of Line: Isle of Mull
Length of Line: 1¼ miles

Gauge: 10¼ inches
Nº of Steam Locos: 2
Nº of Other Locos: 2
Nº of Members: 30
Annual Membership Fee: £5.00
Approx Nº of Visitors P.A.: 30,000
Web site: www.mullrail.co.uk

GENERAL INFORMATION

Nearest Mainline Station: Oban (11 miles by Cal-Mac Ferry)
Nearest Bus Station: Oban (as above)
Car Parking: Free parking on site at Craignure
Coach Parking: Free parking at site
Souvenir Shop(s): Yes
Food & Drinks: No – but drinks & sweets available

SPECIAL INFORMATION

This narrow gauge railway was the first passenger railway to be built on a Scottish island. It was built specially to link Torosay Castle & Gardens to the main Port of entry at Craignure.

OPERATING INFORMATION

Opening Times: Daily from 20th March to 25th October. Open from 11.00am to 5.00pm.
Steam Working: Steam and diesel trains are run depending on operational requirements.
Prices: Adult Single £3.75; Adult Return £4.75
Child Single £2.25; Adult Return £3.25
Family Tickets (2 adults + 2 children)
Single £9.50; Return £14.00
Note: Joint Ferry, Train & Castle tickets are available for purchase at Craignure. Other special rates for large groups and for Children are also available.

Detailed Directions by Car:
Once off the ferry, turn left at the end of the pier, go straight on for almost ½ mile then turn left at the thistle sign opposite the Police station and carry straight on until you reach the station car park.

NEWBY HALL MINIATURE RAILWAY

Address: Newby Hall & Gardens, near Ripon HG4 5AE **Telephone Nº**: (01423) 322583 **Year Formed**: 1971 **Location of Line**: Newby Hall, Ripon **Length of Line**: Approximately 1 mile	**Nº of Steam Locos**: 1 **Nº of Other Locos**: 2 **Nº of Members**: None **Approx Nº of Passengers P.A.**: 60,000 **Gauge**: 10¼ inches **Web site**: www.newbyhall.com

GENERAL INFORMATION

Nearest Mainline Station: Knaresborough (7 miles)
Nearest Bus Station: Ripon (3 miles)
Car Parking: Free parking available on site
Coach Parking: Available
Souvenir Shop(s): No specific railway souvenirs
Food & Drinks: Available

SPECIAL INFORMATION

The railway is located within the gardens of Newby Hall and the track runs alongside the scenic River Ure.

OPERATING INFORMATION

Opening Times: Open daily from 21st March until 28th September from 11.00am to 5.30pm. Trains operate at regular intervals throughout the day.
Steam Working: It is hoped to recommence steam working during 2008 following an overhaul of the railway's Royal Scot steam locomotive.
Prices: Return Ticket £1.50
Note: The price above is for train rides only. Entrance to the House and Gardens is an additional charge.

Detailed Directions by Car:
From All Parts: Exit the A1(M) at Junction 48 and follow the signs for Newby Hall towards Ripon briefly along the A168. At the Langthorpe roundabout follow the brown tourist signs for Newby Hall (passing under the A1(M)) and the Hall is approximately 2 miles.

NORTH BAY MINIATURE RAILWAY

Address: Peasholm Park Station, Northstead Manor Gardens, Scarborough   YO12 6PF
Year Opened: 1931
Location: Peasholm Park to Scalby Mills
Length of Line: 1 mile

Nº of Steam Locos: None
Nº of Other Locos: 5
Nº of Members: None
Approx Nº of Visitors P.A.: 95,000
Gauge: 20 inches

GENERAL INFORMATION

Nearest Mainline Station: Scarborough
Nearest Bus Station: Scarborough
Car Parking: Adjacent to the railway
Coach Parking: Adjacent to the railway
Souvenir Shop(s): Yes
Food & Drinks: Yes

SPECIAL INFORMATION

The North Bay Miniature Railway was opened in 1931 and operates between Northstead Manor and Scalby Mills for the Sea Life Centre.

OPERATING INFORMATION

Opening Times: Daily from Easter until the end of September then at weekends and local school holidays during the winter. Trains run at varying times, depending on the time of the year. Please phone 07787 967694 for further details.
Steam Working: None
Prices: Adult Return £2.80
        Child Return £2.20

Detailed Directions by Car:
From All Parts: Take the A64, A165 or A170 to Scarborough and follow the signs for North Bay Leisure Park. The railway is situated just off the A165 opposite Peasholm Park. Alternatively, follow signs for the Sea Life Centre for Scalby Mills Station.

NORTH GLOUCESTERSHIRE RAILWAY

Address: The Station, Toddington, Cheltenham, Gloucestershire GL54 5DT **Telephone Nº**: (01242) 621405 **Year Formed**: 1985 **Location of Line**: 5 miles south of Broadway, Worcestershire, near the A46 **Length of Line**: ½ mile	**Nº of Steam Locos**: 4 **Nº of Other Locos**: 5 **Nº of Members**: – **Annual Membership Fee**: – **Approx Nº of Visitors P.A.**: – **Gauge**: 2 feet **Web site**: www.isibutu.pwp.blueyonder.co.uk

GENERAL INFORMATION

Nearest Mainline Station: Cheltenham Spa or Ashchurch
Nearest Bus Station: Cheltenham
Car Parking: Parking available at Toddington, Winchcombe & Cheltenham Racecourse Stations
Coach Parking: Parking available as above
Souvenir Shop(s): Yes
Food & Drinks: Available

SPECIAL INFORMATION

The railway boasts the only German-built World War One Henschel locomotive in this country.

OPERATING INFORMATION

Opening Times: Sundays and Bank Holidays from Easter until the end of August. Also open on 30th September and 1st October. Trains usually run from every 35 minutes from around noon.
Steam Working: Most operating days
Prices: Please contact the railway for details.

Detailed Directions by Car:
Toddington is 11 miles north east of Cheltenham, 5 miles south of Broadway just off the B4632 (old A46). Exit the M5 at Junction 9 towards Stow-on-the-Wold for the B4632. The Railway is clearly visible from the B4632.

NORTH INGS FARM MUSEUM

Address: Fen Road, Dorrington,
Lincoln   LN4 3QB
Telephone Nº: (01526) 833100
Year Formed: 1971
Location of Line: Dorrington
Length of Line: A third of a mile

Nº of Steam Locos: 1
Nº of Other Locos: 8
Approx Nº of Visitors P.A.: –
Gauge: 2 feet
Web site: www.northingsfarmmuseum.co.uk

GENERAL INFORMATION

Nearest Mainline Station: Ruskington (3 miles)
Nearest Bus Station: Dorrington (1 mile)
Car Parking: Free parking available on site
Coach Parking: Free parking available on site
Souvenir Shop(s): None
Food & Drinks: None

SPECIAL INFORMATION

The railway forms part of an agricultural machinery
and tractor museum, originally built to serve the
farm.

OPERATING INFORMATION

Opening Times: The first Sunday of the month
from April through to October inclusive. Open from
10.00am to 5.00pm
Steam Working: Subject to availability. Please
contact the Farm Museum for further information.
Prices: Adult £3.00
Child £1.50

Detailed Directions by Car:
From All Parts: North Ings Farm Museum is situated just off the B1188 between Lincoln and Sleaford. Turn into
Dorrington Village at the Musician's Arms public house, pass through the village and under the railway bridge.
The Museum entrance is on the right after 600 yards and the Museum is then ½ mile down the farm road.

OLD KILN LIGHT RAILWAY

Address: Rural Life Centre, Reeds Road, Tilford, Farnham, Surrey GU10 2DL	**Nº of Steam Locos**: 2
Telephone Nº: (01252) 795571	**Nº of Other Locos**: 10
Year Formed: 1975	**Nº of Members**: 14
Location: 3 miles south of Farnham	**Annual Membership Fee**: £25.00
Length of Line: ¾ mile	**Approx Nº of Visitors P.A.**: 21,000
Web site: www.rural-life.org.uk	**Gauge**: 2 feet

GENERAL INFORMATION

Nearest Mainline Station: Farnham (4 miles)
Nearest Bus Station: Farnham
Car Parking: Free parking available on site
Coach Parking: Free parking available on site
Souvenir Shop(s): Yes
Food & Drinks: Available

SPECIAL INFORMATION

The Railway is part of the Rural Life Centre at Tilford. The Centre contains the biggest country life collection in the South of England with a wide range of attractions. A line extension to ¾ mile has recently been opened.

OPERATING INFORMATION

Opening Times: The Rural Life Centre is open Wednesday to Sunday and Bank Holidays from 15th March to 8th October 10.00am – 5.00pm. Open Wednesdays and Sundays only during the winter 11.00am – 4.00pm. Santa Specials run on 6th, 7th, 13th and 14th December.
Steam Working: Bank Holidays and special events once a month – contact the Centre for details. Also for Santa Specials. Diesel at all other times.
Prices: Steam-hauled rides £1.50
Diesel-hauled rides £1.00

Detailed Directions by Car:
The Rural Life Centre is situated 3 miles south of Farnham. From Farnham take the A287 southwards before turning left at Millbridge crossroads into Reeds Road. The Centre is on the left after about ½ mile, just after the Frensham Garden Centre; From the A3: Turn off at the Hindhead crossroads and head north to Tilford. Pass through Tilford, cross the River Wey then turn left into Reeds Road. The Centre is on the right after ½ mile.

ORCHARD FARM LAKESIDE RAILWAY

Address: Orchard Farm Holiday Village, Hunmanby, Filey YO14 0PU	**No of Steam Locos**: 1
Telephone No: (01723) 891582	**No of Other Locos**: 2
Year Formed: 1995	**Approx No of Visitors P.A.**: Not known
Location of Line: Hunmanby, near Filey	**Gauge**: 10¼ inches
Length of Line: 600 yards	**Web**: www.orchardfarmholidayvillage.co.uk

GENERAL INFORMATION

Nearest Mainline Station: Hunmanby (½ mile)
Nearest Bus Station: Scarborough (8 miles)
Car Parking: Available on site
Coach Parking: Available in Hunmanby villages
Souvenir Shop(s): Yes
Food & Drinks: Available

OPERATING INFORMATION

Opening Times: Weekends and daily during the School Holidays.
Steam Working: None at present. Expected to be available during July and August 2009.
Prices: £1.00 per ride.

Detailed Directions by Car:
Turn off the A165 Scarborough to Bridlington road near Hunmanby Moor and opposite the entrance to the Primrose Valley Holiday Camp. Follow the road for about ½ mile to Hunmanby village. Turn right into the Orchard Farm Holiday site on the outskirts on Hunmanby.

PALLOT STEAM, MOTOR & GENERAL MUSEUM

Address: Rue de Bechet, Trinity, Jersey, JE3 5BE	**Nº of Steam Locos:** 4
Telephone Nº: (01534) 865307	**Nº of Other Locos:** 2
Year Formed: 1990	**Nº of Members:** None
Location of Line: Trinity, Jersey	**Approx Nº of Visitors P.A.:** 12,000
Length of Line: ¼ mile	**Gauge:** Standard and 2 feet
	Web site: www.pallotmuseum.co.uk

GENERAL INFORMATION

Nearest Mainline Station: None
Nearest Bus Station: St. Helier
Car Parking: Available on site
Coach Parking: Available on site
Souvenir Shop(s): Yes
Food & Drinks: Snacks only

SPECIAL INFORMATION

The museum was founded by Lyndon (Don) Pallot who spent his early career as a trainee engineer with the old Jersey Railway.

OPERATING INFORMATION

Opening Times: 2008 Dates: Open daily from 17th March to 31st October. Open from 10.00am to 5.00pm. Closed on Sundays.
Steam Working: On some specialevent days only.
Prices: Adult Museum Admission £4.80
Child Museum Admission £1.50
Senior Citizen Museum Admission £4.30
Adult Train Ride £1.70
Child Train Ride £1.20

Detailed Directions by Car:
The museum lies between the A8 and the A9 main roads (Bus Route 5 is easiest) and is signposted off both of these roads.

PERRYGROVE RAILWAY

Address: Perrygrove Railway, Coleford,
Gloucestershire   GL16 8QB
Telephone Nº: (01594) 834991
Year Formed: 1996
Location of Line: ½ mile south of Coleford
Length of Line: ¾ mile

Nº of Steam Locos: 4 (from Sept. 2008)
Nº of Other Locos: 2
Nº of Members: 2
Approx Nº of Visitors P.A.: Not known
Gauge: 15 inches
Web site: www.perrygrove.co.uk

Photo courtesy of George Harris

GENERAL INFORMATION

Nearest Mainline Station:
Lydney (for Parkend)
Nearest Bus Station:
Bus stops in Coleford
Car Parking:
Free parking available on site
Coach Parking: Free parking on site
Souvenir Shop(s): Yes
Food & Drinks: Sandwiches & light
refreshments are available

SPECIAL INFORMATION

Perrygrove is a unique railway with 4
stations, all with access to private
woodland walks. Lots of picnic tables are
available in the open and under cover.
There is also an indoor village with
secret passages.

OPERATING INFO

Opening Times: Every Saturday and
Sunday from 21st March to 2nd
November and daily throughout the
local school holidays. Halloween Ghost
Trains and Santa Specials also run (pre-
booking is essential for these). Please
phone for further details. Railway opens
at 10.30am with the last train at 4.15pm
or 3.45pm depending on the time of
year.
Steam Working:
Most services are steam-hauled.
Prices: Adult £4.60 (All-day ticket)
           Senior Citizen £4.10
               (All-day ticket)
           Child (ages 3-16) £3.60
               (All-day ticket)

Detailed Directions by Car:
From All Parts: Travel to Coleford, Gloucestershire. Upon reaching the vicinity of Coleford, the Perrygrove Railway
is clearly signposted with brown tourist signs from all directions.

RAVENGLASS & ESKDALE RAILWAY

Address: Ravenglass, Cumbria
CA18 1SW
Telephone Nº: (01229) 717171
Year Formed: 1875
Location: The Lake District National Park
Length of Line: 7 miles

Gauge: 15 inches
Nº of Steam Locos: 6
Nº of Other Locos: 8
Nº of Members: None
Approx Nº of Visitors P.A.: 120,000
Web site: www.ravenglass-railway.co.uk
E-mail: steam@ravenglass-railway.co.uk

GENERAL INFORMATION

Nearest Mainline Station: Ravenglass (adjacent)
Nearest Bus Stop: Ravenglass
Car Parking: Available at both terminals
Coach Parking: At Ravenglass
Souvenir Shop(s): Yes
Food & Drinks: Yes

SPECIAL INFORMATION

From Ravenglass, the Lake District's only coastal village, the line runs through two lovely valleys to the foot of England's highest mountain. A new station and visitor centre featuring Fellbites Café, Scafell Gift Shop and the Eskdale Meeting Room opened at Dalegarth (Eskdale) in 2005.

OPERATING INFORMATION

Opening Times: The service runs daily from the 15th March until the 2nd November inclusive. Trains also run during most weekends in the Winter, around Christmas and at February half-term. Open from 9.00am to 5.00pm (sometimes later during high season).
Steam Working: Most services are steam hauled.
Prices: Adult £10.20
Child £5.10 (Ages 5 to 15)
Under-5s travel free

Detailed Directions by Car:
The railway is situated just off the main A595 Western Lake District road.

RHYL MINIATURE RAILWAY

Address: Marine Lake, Wellington Road, Rhyl	**Nº of Steam Locos**: 5
Telephone Nº: (01352) 759109	**Nº of Other Locos**: 3
Year Formed: 1911	**Nº of Members**: Approximately 50
Location of Line: Rhyl	**Annual Membership Fee**: £7.50
Length of Line: 1 mile	**Approx Nº of Visitors P.A.**: 10,000
	Gauge: 15 inches
	Web site: www.rhylminiaturerailway.co.uk

GENERAL INFORMATION

Nearest Mainline Station: Rhyl (1 mile)
Nearest Bus Station: Rhyl (1 mile)
Car Parking: Car Park near the Railway
Coach Parking: Available nearby
Souvenir Shop(s): Yes
Food & Drinks: Available

SPECIAL INFORMATION

The trust runs the oldest Miniature Railway in the UK. The principal locomotive and train have been operating there since the 1920's.

OPERATING INFORMATION

Opening Times: Every weekend from Easter until the end of September. Also on Bank Holiday Mondays and daily during the School Summer Holidays. Trains run from 11.00am to 4.00pm.
Steam Working: Every Sunday and also Saturdays and Thursdays during the School Summer Holidays.
Prices: Adult £2.00
Child £1.00

Detailed Directions by Car:
From All Parts: The Railway is located behind the west end of Rhyl Promenade.

RIO GRANDE MINIATURE RAILWAY

Address: Saville Bros Garden Centre, Selby Road, Garforth, Leeds LS25 2AQ	**Nº of Steam Locos**: None
Telephone Nº: (0113) 286-2183	**Nº of Other Locos**: 1
Year Formed: 1978	**Nº of Members**: –
Location of Line: A63 Garforth to Selby	**Approx Nº of Visitors P.A.**: 10,500
Length of Line: ½ mile	**Gauge**: 10¼ inches
	Web site: www.klondyke.co.uk

GENERAL INFORMATION

Nearest Mainline Station: Garforth
Nearest Bus Station: Garforth
Car Parking: Available on site
Coach Parking: Available on site
Souvenir Shop(s): No
Food & Drinks: Café on site

SPECIAL INFORMATION

The Rio Grande Train, owned by William Strike Ltd. operates at the Saville Bros. Garden Centre.

OPERATING INFORMATION

Opening Times: Weekends and Bank Holidays from March to September. Trains run from 11.00am to 4.00pm.
Steam Working: None
Prices: Adult Return £1.00
        Child Return £1.00

Detailed Directions by Car:
From the M1 and M62: Take the A1(M) north and exit at Junction 46. Follow the A63 towards Selby and go straight on at the next roundabout with the Old George Pub on the left. Continue straight on up the hill passing the Crusader pub on the left and the Garden Centre is on the left; From the A1: Exit the A1 onto the A63 (Milford Lodge Hotel) and follow signs towards Leeds. Go straight on at the first roundabout and the Garden Centre is on the right after approximately ½ mile.

ROMNEY, HYTHE & DYMCHURCH RAILWAY

Address: New Romney Station, New Romney, Kent TN28 8PL **Telephone Nº**: (01797) 362353 **Year Formed**: 1927 **Location of Line**: Approximately 5 miles west of Folkestone **Length of Line**: 13½ miles	**Nº of Steam Locos**: 11 **Nº of Other Locos**: 5 **Nº of Members**: 2,500 **Annual Membership Fee**: Supporters association – Adult £19.00; Junior £7.50 **Approx Nº of Visitors P.A.**: 160,000 **Gauge**: 15 inches **Web site**: www.rhdr.org.uk

GENERAL INFORMATION

Nearest Mainline Station: Folkestone Central (5 miles) or Rye
Nearest Bus Station: Folkestone (then take bus to Hythe)
Car Parking: Free parking at all major stations
Coach Parking: At New Romney & Dungeness
Souvenir Shop(s): Yes – 4 at various stations
Food & Drinks: 2 Cafes serving food and drinks

SPECIAL INFORMATION

Opened in 1927 as 'The World's Smallest Public Railway'. Now the only 15" gauge tourist main line railway in the world. Double track, 6 stations.

OPERATING INFORMATION

Opening Times: A daily service runs from 21st March to 2nd November. Open at weekends in February, March and late October and for Santa Specials in December. Open daily during School half-terms.
Steam Working: All operational days.
Prices: Depend on length of journey. Maximum fares: Adult £12.00
Child £6.00
Family £34.00 (2 adult + 2 children)

Detailed Directions by Car:
Exit the M20 at Junction 11 then follow signs to Hythe and the brown tourist signs for the railway. Alternatively, Take the A259 to New Romney and follow the brown tourist signs for the railway.

ROYAL VICTORIA RAILWAY

Address: Royal Victoria Country Park, Netley, Southampton SO31 5GA
Telephone Nº: (023) 8045-6246
Year Formed: 1995
Location of Line: Netley
Length of Line: 1 mile

Nº of Steam Locos: 10
Nº of Other Locos: 9
Nº of Members: None
Approx Nº of Visitors P.A.: Not known
Gauge: 10¼ inches
Web site: www.royalvictoriarailway.co.uk

GENERAL INFORMATION

Nearest Mainline Station: Netley
Nearest Bus Station: Southampton
Car Parking: Available on site – £1.20 fee
Coach Parking: Free parking available on site
Souvenir Shop(s): Yes
Food & Drinks: Yes

SPECIAL INFORMATION

The railway runs through the grounds of an old Victorian hospital and has good views of the Solent and the Isle of Wight. The Park covers 200 acres including woodland, grassland, beaches and picnic sites.

OPERATING INFORMATION

Opening Times: Weekends throughout the year and daily during school holidays. Also by appointment for larger parties.
Steam Working: On special event days only. Please phone for further details.
Prices: Adult Return £1.75
Child Return £1.25
Note: Special rates are available for groups of 10 or more when pre-booked. Under-2s travel free.

Detailed Directions by Car:
From All Parts: Exit the M27 at Junction 8 and follow the Brown Tourist signs for the Royal Victoria Country Park. You will reach the Park after approximately 3 miles.

RUDYARD LAKE STEAM RAILWAY

Address: Rudyard Station, Rudyard, Near Leek, Staffordshire ST13 8PF **Telephone Nº**: (01538) 306704 **Year Formed**: 1985 **Location**: Rudyard to Hunthouse Wood **Length of Line**: 1½ miles	**Nº of Steam Locos**: 5 **Nº of Other Locos**: 2 **Nº of Members**: – **Approx Nº of Visitors P.A.**: 35,000 **Gauge**: 10¼ inches **Web site**: www.rudyardlakerailway.co.uk

GENERAL INFORMATION

Nearest Mainline Station: Stoke-on-Trent (10 miles)
Nearest Bus Station: Leek
Car Parking: Free parking at Rudyard Station
Coach Parking: Free parking at Rudyard Station
Souvenir Shop(s): Yes
Food & Drinks: Yes – Cafe at Dam Station

SPECIAL INFORMATION

The Railway runs along the side of the historic Rudyard Lake that gave author Rudyard Kipling his name. A Steamboat also plies the lake at times. "Drive a Steam Train" courses can be booked or bought as a gift with vouchers valid for 9 months.

OPERATING INFORMATION

Opening Times: Every Sunday and Bank Holiday from mid-February to the end of November. Also open on every Saturday from 5th April to 30th September and Monday to Friday from 21st July to 29th August. Santa Specials also run on 13th and 14th December.
Steam Working: All trains are normally steam hauled. Trains run from 11.00am and the last train runs around 4.00pm.
Prices: Adult Return £3.50
Child Return £2.00
A variety of other fares and Day Rover tickets are also available.

Detailed Directions by Car:
From All Parts: Head for Leek then follow the A523 North towards Macclesfield for 1 mile. Follow the brown tourist signs to the B5331 signposted for Rudyard for ½ mile. Pass under the Railway bridge and turn immediately left and go up the ramp to the Station car park.

RUISLIP LIDO RAILWAY

Address: Reservoir Road, Ruislip, Middlesex HA4 7TY	**N° of Steam Locos**: 1
Telephone N°: (01895) 622595	**N° of Other Locos**: 5
Year Formed: 1979	**N° of Members**: 155
Location of Line: Trains travel from Ruislip Lido to Woody Bay	**Annual Membership Fee**: £15.00
	Approx N° of Visitors P.A.: 60,000
	Gauge: 12 inches
Length of Line: 1¼ miles	**Web site**: www.ruisliplidorailway.org

Photo courtesy of Peter Musgrave

GENERAL INFORMATION

Nearest Mainline Station: West Ruislip (2 miles)
Nearest Bus Station: Ruislip Underground Station
Car Parking: Free parking available at the Lido
Coach Parking: Free parking available at the Lido
Souvenir Shop(s): Yes
Food & Drinks: A Beach Cafe is open on weekends and Bank Holidays. A Pub/Restaurant is open daily.

SPECIAL INFORMATION

The steam locomotive, 'Mad Bess' used by Ruislip Lido Railway was actually built by the members over a 12 year period!

OPERATING INFORMATION

Opening Times: Weekends from mid-February to the end of May and also daily during school holidays. Also open on weekends from September to November and on Sundays in December.
Steam Working: Sundays and Bank Holidays from July to the end of September and also Santa Specials.
Prices: Adult Return £2.00 (Single fare £1.80)
Child Return £1.50 (Single fare £1.30)
Family Return £6.00 (Single fare £5.50)
(2 adults + 2 children)

Detailed Directions by Car:
From All Parts: Follow the signs from the A40 and take the A4180 through Ruislip before turning left onto the B469.

SALTBURN MINIATURE RAILWAY

Address: Valley Gardens, Saltburn
Correspondence: 55 High Street West, Redcar TS10 1SF
Telephone Nº: (01642) 502863
Year Formed: 1947
Location of Line: Cat Nab to Forest Halt Stations, Saltburn
Length of Line: ¾ mile

Nº of Steam Locos: Visiting locos only
Nº of Other Locos: 2
Nº of Members: 12
Annual Membership Fee: £1.00
Approx Nº of Visitors P.A.: 12,000
Gauge: 15 inches
Web site:
www.saltburn-miniature-railway.org.uk

GENERAL INFORMATION

Nearest Mainline Station: Saltburn (½ mile)
Nearest Bus Station: Saltburn (½ mile)
Car Parking: Available at Cat Nab Station
Coach Parking: Glen Side (at the top of the bank)
Souvenir Shop(s): At Cat Nab Station
Food & Drinks: None

OPERATING INFORMATION

Opening Times: Weekends and Bank Holidays from Easter until the end of September. Also open Tuesday to Friday during the Summer School Holidays. Trains run from 1.00pm to 5.00pm.
Steam Working: Please contact the railway for details.
Prices: Adult Return £2.00 (Adult Single £1.00)
Child Return 1.00 (Child Single 50p)
Note: Family tickets and frequent user discounts are also available.

Detailed Directions by Car:
Follow the A174 from Middlesbrough (West) or Whitby (East) to Saltburn-by-the-Sea. Cat Nab Station with its adjoining car park is situated by the beach, directly off the A174.

SHERWOOD FOREST RAILWAY

Address: Sherwood Forest Farm Park, Edwinstowe, Mansfield NG21 9HL	**Nº of Steam Locos**: 2
Telephone Nº: (01623) 515339	**Nº of Other Locos**: 3
Year Formed: 1999	**Nº of Members**: 13
Location of Line: Between Mansfield Woodhouse and Edwinstowe	**Annual Membership Fee**: –
	Approx Nº of Visitors P.A.: 17,000
Length of Line: 680 yards	**Gauge**: 15 inches
	Web site: www.sherwoodforestrailway.com

GENERAL INFORMATION

Nearest Mainline Station: Mansfield (7 miles)
Nearest Bus Station: Mansfield (7 miles)
Car Parking: Free parking available on site
Coach Parking: Available on site
Souvenir Shop(s): Yes
Food & Drinks: Available

SPECIAL INFORMATION

The Railway runs through the grounds of a 26 acre Farm Park which contains hundreds of rare breeds of animals, terraced flower gardens, a small petting area and play areas for children.

OPERATING INFORMATION

Opening Times: Daily from Good Friday until the 28th September. The Farm Park is open from 10.30am but trains run from 12.00pm to 5.00pm.
Steam Working: Every operating day
Prices: Adults £1.00 (Allows rides for a month)
Chidren £1.00 (Allows rides for a month)
Family £4.00 (Allows rides for a month)
Farm Park Entrance Charges:
Adults £6.50
Concessions £5.50
Children £4.50 (Under 3s admitted free)
Family £20.00

Detailed Directions by Car:
From the A1: Turn off at the Worksop roundabout and head to Ollerton. Follow the A6075 through Edwinstowe and towards Mansfield Woodhouse, then turn left at the double mini-roundabout. The Farm Park is on the right after approximately 200 yards; From Nottingham: Head to Ollerton, then as above; From the M1: Exit at Junction 27 and head into Mansfield. Follow signs to Mansfield Woodhouse and then on towards Edwinstowe. From here, follow the tourist signs for the Farm Park.

SITTINGBOURNE & KEMSLEY LIGHT RAILWAY

Address: P.O. Box 300, Sittingbourne, Kent ME10 2DZ
Bookings: (0871) 222-1569 (Evenings)
Info/Talking Timetable: (0871) 222-1568
Year Formed: 1969
Location of Line: North of Sittingbourne
Length of Line: 2 miles

N° of Steam Locos: 9 (2 Standard gauge)
N° of Other Locos: 3
N° of Members: 350
Annual Membership Fee: £15.00
Approx N° of Visitors P.A.: 7,500
Gauge: 2 feet 6 inches
Web site: www.sklr.net

GENERAL INFORMATION

Nearest Mainline Station: Sittingbourne (¼ mile)
Nearest Bus Station: Sittingbourne Mainline station
Car Parking: Sittingbourne Retail Park (behind McDonalds)
Coach Parking: Sittingbourne Retail Park
Souvenir Shop(s): Yes
Food & Drinks: Yes

SPECIAL INFORMATION

The railway is the only original preserved narrow gauge industrial steam railway in S.E. England (formerly the Bowaters Paper Company Railway). The railway celebrated 100 years of Steam locomotion in 2005 and the line includes a trip along a ½ mile concrete viaduct. Other attractions include a Museum, Model Railways, a Children's play area and a Wildlife Garden.

OPERATING INFORMATION

Opening Times: Sundays and Bank Holiday weekends from April to September. Also open on Wednesdays in the School holidays and for Santa Specials on certain dates in December. Phone for details of Special Events held throughout the year.
Steam Working: Trains run from 1.00pm normally, but from 11.00am on Bank Holiday weekends and Sundays in August. Last train runs at 4.00pm (except for during some special events). Diesel services occasionally run on mornings.
Prices: Adult Return £5.00   Child Return £2.50
Senior Citizen Return £3.50   Family Return £14.00
Note: Different fares may apply on special event days.

Detailed Directions by Car:
From East or West: Take the M2 (or M20) to A249 and travel towards Sittingbourne. Take the A2 to Sittingbourne town and continue to the roundabout outside the Mainline station. Take the turning onto the B2006 (Milton Regis) under the Mainline bridge and the car park entrance for the Railway is by the next roundabout, behind McDonalds, in the Sittingbourne Retail Park.

SNOWDON MOUNTAIN RAILWAY

Address: Llanberis, Caernarfon, Gwynedd, Wales LL55 4TY	**Length of Line:** 4¾ miles
Telephone Nº: (0871) 720-0033	**Nº of Steam Locos:** 4
Fax Nº: (01286) 872518	**Nº of Other Locos:** 4
Year Formed: 1894	**Nº of Members:** –
Location of Line: Llanberis to Snowdon summit	**Approx Nº of Visitors P.A.:** 140,000
	Gauge: 2 feet 7½ inches
	Web site: www.snowdonrailway.co.uk

GENERAL INFORMATION

Nearest Mainline Station: Bangor (9 miles)
Nearest Bus Station: Caernarfon (7½ miles)
Car Parking: Llanberis Station car park – pay and display. Also other car parks nearby.
Coach Parking: As above but space is very limited
Souvenir Shop(s): Yes
Food & Drinks: Yes

SPECIAL INFORMATION

Britain's only public rack and pinion mountain railway climbs to withing 60 feet of the 3,560 feet peak of Snowdon, Wales' highest mountain. The round trip to Clogwyn takes approximately 2 hours and includes a 30 minute stop at the summit. In the event of poor weather trains run to Clogwyn or Rocky Valley where a partial fare applies.

OPERATING INFORMATION

Opening Times: 2008 dates: Open daily (weather permitting) from 15th March to the first week of November. Trains run every 30 minutes (subject to public demand) from 9.00am until mid/late afternoon. The last departure can be as late as 5.00pm depending on demand. It is advisable to book in advance during school holidays.
Steam Working: Most days but subject to engine availability and daily traffic plan.
Prices: Adult Summit Return £22.00
Child Summit Return £15.00
Special rates are available for large groups. Please phone 0870 458-0033 for further details.

Detailed Directions by Car:
Llanberis Station is situated on the A4086 Caernarfon to Capel Curig road, 7½ miles from Caernarfon. Convenient access via the main North Wales coast road (A55). Exit at the A55/A5 junction and follow signs to Llanberis via B4366, B4547 and A4086.

SOUTH DOWNS LIGHT RAILWAY

Address: South Downs Light Railway, Stopham Road, Pulborough RH20 1DS
Telephone Nº: (07711) 717470
Year Formed: 1999
Location: Pulborough Garden Centre
Length of Line: 1 kilometre

Nº of Steam Locos: 10
Nº of Other Locos: 2
Nº of Members: 60
Annual Membership Fee: Adult £20.00
Approx Nº of Visitors P.A.: 15,000
Gauge: 10¼ inches
Web site: www.sdlrs.com

GENERAL INFORMATION

Nearest Mainline Station: Pulborough (½ mile)
Nearest Bus Station: Bus stop just outside Centre
Car Parking: Free parking on site
Coach Parking: Free parking on site
Souvenir Shop(s): Yes
Food & Drinks: Yes – in the Garden Restaurant

SPECIAL INFORMATION

The members of the Society own and operate the largest collection of 10¼ inch gauge scale locomotives in the UK. The Railway is sited in the Wyevale Garden Centre.

OPERATING INFORMATION

Opening Times: Weekends and Bank Holidays from March until September and also Santa Specials at weekends in December. Trains run from 11.00am to 3.30pm.
Steam Working: Most services are steam hauled.
Prices: Adult £1.50
Child £1.00 (Under-2s travel free of charge)
Note: Supersaver tickets are also available.

Detailed Directions by Car:
From All Parts: The Centre is situated on the A283, ½ mile west of Pulborough. Pulborough itself is on the A29 London to Bognor Regis Road.

SOUTH TYNEDALE RAILWAY

Address: The Railway Station, Alston, Cumbria   CA9 3JB
Telephone Nº: (01434) 381696 (Enquiries) (01434) 382828 (Talking timetable)
Year Formed: 1973
Location of Line: From Alston, northwards along South Tyne Valley to Kirkhaugh

Length of Line: 2¼ miles
Nº of Steam Locos: 5
Nº of Other Locos: 5
Nº of Members: 290
Annual Membership Fee: £15.00
Approx Nº of Visitors P.A.: 22,000
Gauge: 2 feet
Web site: www.strps.org.uk

GENERAL INFORMATION

Nearest Mainline Station: Haltwhistle (15 miles)
Nearest Bus Station: Alston Townfoot (¼ mile)
Car Parking: Free parking at Alston Station
Coach Parking: Free parking at Alston Station
Souvenir Shop(s): Yes
Food & Drinks: Yes

OPERATING INFORMATION

Opening Times: Bank Holidays and Weekends from 21st March until the end of October. Open daily from 19th July to 7th September. Also open Tuesdays and Thursdays in June and September. Please contact the Railway for further details.
Steam Working: Varies, but generally weekends and Bank Holidays throughout Summer & December.
Prices: Adult Return £5.50;   Adult Single £3.30
Child Return £2.50;   Child Single £1.50
Family Return Ticket £15.00
Children under 3 travel free
Adult All Day Ticket £9.00
Child All Day Ticket £4.00

Detailed Directions by Car:
Alston can be reached by a number of roads from various directions including A689, A686 and the B6277. Alston Station is situated just off the A686 Hexham road, north of Alston Town Centre. Look for the brown tourist signs on roads into Alston.

STAPLEFORD MINIATURE RAILWAY

Address: Stapleford Park, Stapleford, Melton Mowbray, Leicestershire
Telephone Nº: (01949) 860138
Year Formed: 1957
Location of Line: Stapleford Park
Length of Line: 2 miles
Web site: www.fsmr.org.uk

Nº of Steam Locos: 5
Nº of Other Locos: 1
Nº of Members: 45
Annual Membership Fee: By invitation
Approx Nº of Visitors P.A.: Not known
Gauge: 10¼ inches

GENERAL INFORMATION

Nearest Mainline Station: Melton Mowbray (4 miles)
Nearest Bus Station: Melton Mowbray (4 miles)
Car Parking: Available on site
Coach Parking: Available on site
Souvenir Shop(s): Yes
Food & Drinks: Available – including a licensed bar

SPECIAL INFORMATION

The railway is only open to the public for two weekends a year as shown. The June event is run in conjunction with a Steam Rally and various traction engines will be on site. The August event concentrates on the railway with other smaller attractions. Weekend camping is available at both events. Please check the web site for details.

OPERATING INFORMATION

Opening Times: 2008 dates: 14th and 15th June, 24th and 25th August.
Steam Working: All trains on the open weekends
Prices: Adult £2.00
          Child £2.00
Note: Family Tickets are also available

Detailed Directions by Car:
The railway is located off the B676 Melton Mowbray to Colsterworth road about 4 miles to the East of Melton Mowbray. The Stapleford Park Hotel is well-signposted with brown tourist signs and follow these to turn off the B676. The railway is located on the left hand side just before Stapleford Village and the turn into the hotel.

STEEPLE GRANGE LIGHT RAILWAY

Contact Address: 4 Oak Tree Gardens, Tansley, Matlock DE4 5WA **Telephone Nº**: (01629) 580917 **Year Formed**: 1986 **Location of Line**: Off the High Peak trail near Wirksworth **Length of Line**: ½ mile at present	**Nº of Steam Locos**: 1 (awaiting rebuild) **Nº of Other Locos**: 17 **Nº of Members**: 150 **Annual Membership Fee**: From £6.00 **Approx Nº of Visitors P.A.**: 8,000+ **Gauge**: 18 inches **Web site**: www.steeplegrange.co.uk

GENERAL INFORMATION

Nearest Mainline Station: Cromford (2 miles)
Nearest Bus Station: Matlock
Car Parking: Free parking available nearby
Coach Parking: Free parking available nearby
Souvenir Shop(s): Yes
Food & Drinks: Light refreshments available

SPECIAL INFORMATION

The Railway is built on the track bed of the former Standard Gauge Cromford and High Peak Railway branch to Middleton. The railway uses mostly former mining/quarrying rolling stock.

OPERATING INFORMATION

Opening Times: Sundays and Bank Holidays from Easter until the end of October. Also open on Saturdays from July to September and by prior arrangement. Special Events at other times of the year including Santa Specials on the 2nd weekend in December. Trains run from 12.00pm to 5.00pm
Steam Working: None at present
Prices: Adult Return £1.50
　　　　　　Child Return 50p
　　　　　　Family Return £4.00 (2 Adult + 3 Child)
Note: Special fares apply during special events and also for group bookings.

Detailed Directions by Car:
The Railway is situated adjacent to the National Stone Centre just to the north of Wirksworth at the junction of the B5035 and B5036. Free car parking is available at the National Stone Centre and in Old Porter Lane.

SUTTON HALL RAILWAY

Address: Tabors Farm, Sutton Hall, Shopland Road, near Rochford, Essex SS4 1LQ	**Nº of Steam Locos**: 1
	Nº of Other Locos: 1
Telephone Nº: (01702) 334337	**Nº of Members**: Approximately 8
Year Formed: 1997	**Annual Membership Fee**: £15.00
Location of Line: Sutton Hall Farm	**Approx Nº of Visitors P.A.**: 3,500
Length of Line: Almost 1 mile	**Gauge**: 10¼ inches
	Web site: www.suttonhallrailway.com

GENERAL INFORMATION

Nearest Mainline Station: Rochford (1½ miles)
Nearest Bus Station: Rochford
Car Parking: Free parking available on site
Coach Parking: Free parking available on site
Souvenir Shop(s): None
Food & Drinks: Drinks and snacks available

SPECIAL INFORMATION

The Railway was bought by C. Tabor in 1985 for use with his Farm Barn Dances. The Sutton Hall Railway Society was formed in 1997 (with C. Tabor as Society President) and now opens the line for public running on some Sundays. The railway is staffed entirely by Volunteer Members of the Society.

OPERATING INFORMATION

Opening Times: Open the 4th Sunday in the month from April until September, 12.00pm to 6.00pm. Specials run on Easter Sunday afternoon, Halloween evening and a Santa Special on the 2nd Sunday in December.
Steam Working: All operating days.
Prices: Adult Return £2.00
            Child Return £1.50

Detailed Directions by Car:
From Southend Airport (A127 Southend to London Main Route & A1159): At the Airport Roundabout (with the McDonalds on the left) go over the railway bridge signposted for Rochford. At the 1st roundabout turn right (Ann Boleyn Pub on the right) into Sutton Road. Continue straight on at the mini-roundabout then when the road forks turn left into Shopland Road signposted for Barling and Great Wakering. Turn right after approximately 400 yards into the long tree-lined road for Sutton Hall Farm.

TALYLLYN RAILWAY

Address: Wharf Station, Tywyn, Gwynedd, LL36 9EY	**N⁰ of Steam Locos**: 6
Telephone N⁰: (01654) 710472	**N⁰ of Other Locos**: 4
Year Formed: 1865	**N⁰ of Members**: 3,500
Location of Line: Tywyn to Nant Gwernol Station	**Annual Membership Fee**: Adult £25.00
	Approx N⁰ of Visitors P.A.: 50,000
Length of Line: 7¼ miles	**Gauge**: 2 feet 3 inches
	Web site: www.talyllyn.co.uk

GENERAL INFORMATION

Nearest Mainline Station: Tywyn (300 yards)
Nearest Bus Station: Tywyn (300 yards)
Car Parking: 100 yards away
Coach Parking: Free parking (100 yards)
Souvenir Shop(s): Yes
Food & Drinks: Yes

SPECIAL INFORMATION

Talyllyn Railway was the first preserved railway in the world – saved from closure in 1951. The railway was originally opened in 1866 to carry slate from Bryn Eglwys Quarry to Tywyn. Among the railway's attractions are a Narrow Gauge Railway Museum at the Tywyn Wharf terminus.

OPERATING INFORMATION

Opening Times: Daily from 16th March to 8th November. Generally open from 10.00am to 5.00pm (later during the summer). Also open for Santa/New Year Specials on some dates in December/January.
Steam Working: All services are steam-hauled.
Prices: Adult Return £12.00 (Day Rover ticket) Children (ages 5-15) pay £2.00 if travelling with an adult. Otherwise, they pay half adult fare. Children under the age of 5 travel free of charge.
The fares shown above are for a full round trip. Tickets to intermediate stations are cheaper.

Detailed Directions by Car:
From the North: Take the A493 from Dolgellau into Tywyn; From the South: Take the A493 from Machynlleth to Tywyn.

TEIFI VALLEY RAILWAY

Address: Henllan Station, Henllan, near Newcastle Emlyn, Carmarthenshire **Telephone Nº**: (01559) 371077 **Year Formed**: 1978 **Location of Line**: Between Cardigan and Carmarthen off the A484 **Length of Line**: 2 miles	**Nº of Steam Locos**: 2 **Nº of Other Locos**: 3 **Nº of Members**: Approximately 150 **Annual Membership Fee**: £12.00 **Approx Nº of Visitors P.A.**: 15,000 **Gauge**: 2 feet **Web site**: www.teifivalleyrailway.com

GENERAL INFORMATION

Nearest Mainline Station: Carmarthen (10 miles)
Nearest Bus Station: Carmarthen (10 miles)
Car Parking: Spaces for 70 cars available.
Coach Parking: Spaces for 4 coaches available.
Souvenir Shop(s): Yes
Food & Drinks: Yes (snacks only)

SPECIAL INFORMATION

The Railway was formerly part of the G.W.R. but now runs on a Narrow Gauge using Quarry Engines.

OPERATING INFORMATION

Opening Times: Open daily from 17th March until the end of September (closed some Fridays). Open on weekends in October and daily from 25th to 31st October. Also open on some days in December for 'Santa Specials'. Trains run from 11.00am – 4.30pm.
Steam Working: Most operating days – please phone the Railway for further details.
Prices: Adult £5.50
Child £3.50
Senior Citizen £5.00
A 10% discount is available for parties of 10 or more.

Detailed Directions by Car:
From All Parts: The Railway is situated in the Village of Henllan between the A484 and the A475 (on the B4334) about 4 miles east of Newcastle Emlyn.

VALE OF RHEIDOL RAILWAY

Address: The Locomotive Shed, Park Avenue, Aberystwyth, Dyfed SY23 1PG	**Nº of Steam Locos**: 3
Telephone Nº: (01970) 625819	**Nº of Other Locos**: 1
Year Formed: 1902	**Nº of Members**: None
Location of Line: Aberystwyth to Devil's Bridge	**Annual Membership Fee**: –
	Approx Nº of Visitors P.A.: 38,000
Length of Line: 11¾ miles	**Gauge**: 1 foot 11¾ inches
	Web site: www.rheidolrailway.co.uk

GENERAL INFORMATION

Nearest Mainline Station: Aberystwyth (adjacent)
Nearest Bus Station: Aberystwyth (adjacent)
Car Parking: Available on site
Coach Parking: Parking available 400 yards away
Souvenir Shop(s): Yes
Food & Drinks: Yes

SPECIAL INFORMATION

The journey between the stations take one hour in each direction. At Devil's Bridge there is a cafe, toilets, a picnic area and the famous Mynach Falls. The line climbs over 600 feet in 11¾ miles.

OPERATING INFORMATION

Opening Times: Open almost every day from 21st March to 30th October 2008 with some exceptions. Please phone the railway for further information.
Steam Working: All trains are steam-hauled. Trains run from 10.30am to 4.00pm on most days.
Prices: Adult Return £13.50
          Child Return – First 2 children per adult pay £3.00 each. Further children pay £6.75 each

---

Detailed Directions by Car:
From the North take A487 into Aberystwyth. From the East take A470 and A44 to Aberystwyth. From the South take A487 or A485 to Aberystwyth. The Station is joined on to the Mainline Station in Alexandra Road.

VANSTONE PARK MINIATURE RAILWAY

Address: Vanstone Park Garden Centre, Hitchin Road, near Codicote SG4 8TH	**N° of Steam Locos**: None
Telephone N°: (01438) 820412	**N° of Other Locos**: 4
Year Formed: 1986	**N° of Members**: None
Location: Vanstone Park Garden Centre	**Approx N° of Visitors P.A.**: Not known
Length of Line: 600 yards	**Gauge**: 10¼ inches

GENERAL INFORMATION

Nearest Mainline Station: Knebworth
Nearest Bus Station: Hitchin
Car Parking: Available on site
Coach Parking: Available on site
Souvenir Shop(s): Yes
Food & Drinks: Yes

SPECIAL INFORMATION

The Railway runs through the Vanstone Park Garden Centre.

OPERATING INFORMATION

Opening Times: Weekends and Bank Holidays throughout the year, weather permitting. Santa Specials run on weekends during December. Please phone to avoid disappointment. Trains run from 11.00am to 4.30pm
Steam Working: None
Prices: Adult Return £1.60
Child Return £1.00

Detailed Directions by Car:
From All Parts: Exit the A1(M) at Junction 6 and take the B656. Vanstone Park is just off the B656 one mile to the north of Codicote.

WATERWORKS RAILWAY

<table>
<tr><td>Address: Kew Bridge Steam Museum, Green Dragon Lane, Brentford   TW8 0EN
Telephone N°: (020) 8568-4757
Year Formed: 1986
Location of Line: Greater London
Length of Line: Under 1 mile</td><td>N° of Steam Locos: 1
N° of Other Locos: 1
N° of Members: 750
Annual Membership Fee: £20.00 Adult
Approx N° of Visitors P.A.: 20,000
Gauge: Narrow</td></tr>
</table>

GENERAL INFORMATION

Nearest Mainline Station: Kew Bridge (3 minute walk)
Nearest Bus Station: Bus stop across the road – Services 65, 267 and 237
Car Parking: Spaces for 43 cars available on site
Coach Parking: Available on site – book in advance
Souvenir Shop(s): Yes
Food & Drinks: Yes – at weekends only

SPECIAL INFORMATION

The Museum is a former Victorian Pumping Station with a collection of working Steam Pumping Engines. The Railway demonstrates typical water board use of Railways.

OPERATING INFORMATION

Opening Times: 11.00am to 4.00pm, from Tuesday to Sunday inclusive throughout the year (closed on Mondays except for Bank Holidays).
Steam Working: Sundays and Bank Holiday Mondays from March to November.
Prices: Adult £8.50
             Child – Free if accompanied by Adults
             Senior Citizen £7.50

Web site: www.kbsm.org

Detailed Directions by Car:
From All Parts: Exit the M4 at Junction 2 and follow the A4 to Chiswick Roundabout. Take the exit signposted for Kew Gardens & Brentford. Go straight on at the next two sets of traffic lights following A315. After 2nd set of lights take the first right for the museum. The museum is next to the tall Victorian tower.

WELLS HARBOUR RAILWAY

Address: Wells Harbour Railway, Beach Road, Wells-next-the-Sea NR23 1DR **Telephone Nº**: (07939) 149264 **Year Formed**: 1976 **Location of Line**: Wells-next-the-Sea **Length of Line**: Approximately 1 mile	**Nº of Steam Locos**: 1 **Nº of Other Locos**: 2 **Nº of Members**: None **Approx Nº of Visitors P.A.**: 50,000 **Gauge**: 10¼ inches **Web site**: www.wellsharbourrailway.com

GENERAL INFORMATION

Nearest Mainline Station: King's Lynn (21 miles)
Nearest Bus Station: Norwich (24 miles)
Car Parking: Public car parks near each station
Coach Parking: Available in town
Souvenir Shop(s): No
Food & Drinks: No

SPECIAL INFORMATION

Wells Harbour Railway was the first 10¼" narrow gauge railway to run a scheduled passenger service and is listed in the Guinness Book of Records!

OPERATING INFORMATION

Opening Times: Weekends from Easter until Spring Bank Holiday then daily through to the middle of September. Then weekends until the end of October. The first train departs at 10.30am.
Steam Working: None
Prices: Adult Single £1.20
Child Single £1.00

Detailed Directions by Car:
Wells-next-the-Sea is located on the North Norfolk cost between Hunstanton and Cromer. The railway is situated on Beach Road next to the harbour. Follow the signs for Pinewoods and Beach.

WELLS & WALSINGHAM LIGHT RAILWAY

Address: The Station, Wells-next-the-Sea NR23 1QB	**Nº of Steam Locos:** 1
Telephone Nº: (01328) 711630	**Nº of Other Locos:** 2
Year Formed: 1982	**Nº of Members:** 50
Location of Line: Wells-next-the-Sea to Walsingham, Norfolk	**Annual Membership Fee:** £11.00
	Approx Nº of Visitors P.A.: 20,000
Length of Line: 4 miles	**Gauge:** 10¼ inches

GENERAL INFORMATION

Nearest Mainline Station: King's Lynn (21 miles)
Nearest Bus Station: Norwich (24 miles)
Car Parking: Free parking at site
Coach Parking: Free parking at site
Souvenir Shop(s): Yes
Food & Drinks: Yes

SPECIAL INFORMATION

The Railway is the longest 10¼ inch narrow-gauge steam railway in the world. The course of the railway is famous for wildlife and butterflies in season.

OPERATING INFORMATION

Opening Times: Daily from 21st April until the end of October.
Steam Working: Trains run from 10.15am on operating days.
Prices: Adult Return £7.50
Child Return £6.00

Detailed Directions by Car:
Wells-next-the-Sea is situated on the North Norfolk Coast midway between Hunstanton and Cromer. The Main Station is situated on the main A149 Stiffkey Road. Follow the brown tourist signs for the Railway.

WELSH HIGHLAND RAILWAY (CAERNARFON)

Postal Address: Ffestiniog Railway, Harbour Station, Porthmadog LL49 9NF
Telephone N°: (01766) 516000
Year Formed: 1997
Location: Caernarfon to Rhyd Ddu
Length of Line: 12 miles

N° of Steam Locos: 5 (2 working)
N° of Other Locos: 2
N° of Members: 1,000
Annual Membership Fee: £25.00
Approx N° of Visitors P.A.: 50,000
Gauge: 1 foot 11½ inches
Web site: www.festrail.co.uk

GENERAL INFORMATION

Nearest Mainline Station: Bangor (7 miles) (Bus service N° 5 runs to Caernarfon)
Nearest Bus Station: Caernarfon
Car Parking: Parking available at Caernarfon
Coach Parking: At Victoria Docks (¼ mile)
Souvenir Shop(s): Yes
Food & Drinks: Light refreshments on most trains

SPECIAL INFORMATION

The Railway is being reconstructed between Caernarfon and Porthmadog along the track bed of the original Welsh Highland Railway. Please check the Railway web site for up to date information.

OPERATING INFORMATION

Opening Times: Daily from 15th March to 31st October 2008. There is also a limited service in the Winter. Train times vary depending on the date. Please contact the railway for further information.
Steam Working: Most trains in are steam-hauled.
Prices: Adult £17.50 (All-day Rover ticket)
One child travels free with each adult, additional children travel for half the fare.
Reductions are available for Senior Citizens, Families and groups of 20 or more. Single fares are cheaper than Day Rover tickets.

Detailed Directions by Car:
Take either the A487(T), the A4085 or the A4086 to Caernarfon then follow the brown tourist signs for the Railway which is situated in St. Helens Road next to the Castle.

WELSH HIGHLAND RAILWAY (PORTHMADOG)

Address: Tremadog Road, Porthmadog, Gwynedd LL49 9DY **Telephone Nº:** (01766) 513402 **Year Formed:** 1964 **Location of Line:** Porthmadog, Gwynedd LL49 9DY **Length of Line:** 1½ miles	**Nº of Steam Locos:** 5 **Nº of Other Locos:** 20 **Nº of Members:** 1,000 **Annual Membership Fee:** £25.00 Adult **Approx Nº of Visitors P.A.:** 20,000 **Gauge:** 1 foot 11½ inches **Web site:** www.whr.co.uk

GENERAL INFORMATION

Nearest Mainline Station: Porthmadog (100 yards)
Nearest Bus Station: Services 1 & 3 stop 50 yards away
Car Parking: Free parking at site, plus a public car park within 100 yards
Coach Parking: Adjacent
Souvenir Shop(s): Yes – large range available.
Food & Drinks: Yes – excellent home cooking!

SPECIAL INFORMATION

The Welsh Highland Railway is a family-orientated attraction based around a Railway Heritage Centre and includes a guided, hands-on tour of the sheds. A ¾ mile extension to Traeth Mawr is now open.

OPERATING INFORMATION

Opening Times: Daily from 15th March to 2nd November (closed on Mondays and Fridays during the first 3 weeks of October). Trains run at 10.30am, 11.30am, 1.00pm, 2.00pm, 3.00pm and 4.00pm (the last train runs at 3.00pm during October and November).
Steam Working: 22-30 March; 3/4/5/24-31 May; 1st June; 5/6/12/13/19-31 July; daily in August; weekends in September; 25th October to 2nd November.
Prices: Adult Day Rover £5.50
Child Day Rover £3.00 (Under-5s free)
Senior Citizen Day Rover £4.50
Family Day Rover £15.00
(2 adults + 2 children)

Detailed Directions by Car:
From Bangor/Caernarfon take the A487 to Porthmadog. From Pwllheli take the A497 to Porthmadog then turn left at the roundabout. From the Midlands take A487 to Portmadog. Once in Porthmadog, follow the brown tourist signs. The line is located right next to Porthmadog Mainline Station.

Welshpool & Llanfair Light Railway

Address: The Station, Llanfair Caereinion, Powys SY21 0SF	**N° of Steam Locos**: 9
Telephone N°: (01938) 810441	**N° of Other Locos**: 4
Year Formed: 1959	**N° of Members**: 1,800
Location of Line: Welshpool to Llanfair Caereinion, Mid Wales	**Annual Membership Fee**: £22.50
	Approx N° of Visitors P.A.: 26,000
	Gauge: 2 feet 6 inches
Length of Line: 8 miles	**Web site**: www.wllr.org.uk

GENERAL INFORMATION

Nearest Mainline Station: Welshpool (1 mile)
Nearest Bus Station: Welshpool (1 mile)
Car Parking: Free parking at Welshpool and Llanfair Caereinion
Coach Parking: As above
Souvenir Shop(s): Yes – at both ends of line
Food & Drinks: Yes – at Llanfair only

SPECIAL INFORMATION

The railway has the steepest gradient of any British railway, reaching a summit of 603 feet.

OPERATING INFORMATION

Opening Times: Easter and Bank Holidays and weekends from 21st March to 2nd November. Daily from 19th July to 31st August. Most other days in June and July plus dates in September, October and December. Generally open from 9.30am to 5.00pm.
Steam Working: All trains are steam-hauled
Prices: Adult £11.20
Senior Citizens £10.20
Children under the age of 3 travel free of charge. The first child aged 3-15 per adult also travels free. All other children are charged half-price – £5.60

Detailed Directions by Car:
Both stations are situated alongside the A458 Shrewsbury to Dolgellau road and are clearly signposted

WEST LANCASHIRE LIGHT RAILWAY

Address: Station Road, Hesketh Bank, Nr. Preston, Lancashire PR4 6SP **Telephone N°**: (01772) 815881 **Year Formed**: 1967 **Location of Line**: On former site of Alty's Brickworks, Hesketh Bank **Length of Line**: ¼ mile	**N° of Steam Locos**: 8 **N° of Other Locos**: 25 **N° of Members**: Approximately 105 **Annual Membership Fee**: £15.00 Adult; £20.00 Family **Approx N° of Visitors P.A.**: 14,500 **Gauge**: 2 feet **Web site**: www.westlancs.org

GENERAL INFORMATION

Nearest Mainline Station: Rufford (4 miles)
Nearest Bus Station: Preston (7 miles)
Car Parking: Space for 50 cars at site
Coach Parking: Space for 3 coaches at site
Souvenir Shop(s): Yes
Food & Drinks: Only soft drinks & snacks

SPECIAL INFORMATION

The Railway is run by volunteers and there is a large collection of Industrial Narrow Gauge equipment.

OPERATING INFORMATION

Opening Times: Sundays and Bank Holidays throughout the year. No trains run from November to April (except Santa Specials). Various other Special Events are held during the Summer – phone for details or check the Railway's web site listed above. Trains run from 12.00pm to 5.20pm

Steam Working: Trains operate on Sundays and Bank Holidays from April until the end of October. There are also 'Santa Specials' on the two weekends prior to Christmas.

Prices: Adult £2.50   Child £1.50
Family Tickets £6.00
Senior Citizens £2.00

Detailed Directions by Car:
Travel by the A59 from Liverpool or Preston or by the A565 from Southport to the junction of the two roads at Tarleton. From here follow signs to Hesketh Bank. The Railway is signposted.

WICKSTEED PARK RAILWAY

Address: Wicksteed Park, Kettering, NN15 6NJ **Telephone Nº**: 08700 621194 **Year Formed**: 1931 **Location of Line**: Wicksteed Park **Length of Line**: 1¼ miles	**Nº of Steam Locos**: None **Nº of Other Locos**: 3 **Approx Nº of Visitors P.A.**: 180,000 **Gauge**: 2 feet **Web site**: www.wicksteedpark.co.uk

GENERAL INFORMATION

Nearest Mainline Station: Kettering (2 miles)
Nearest Bus Station: Kettering (2 miles)
Car Parking: Available on site (£6.00 entrance fee per car)
Coach Parking: Free parking available on site
Souvenir Shop(s): Yes
Food & Drinks: Available

SPECIAL INFORMATION

The Railway runs through the grounds of a large leisure complex, Wicksteed Park, which also houses many other attractions including a fairground, a rollercoaster and a log chute ride.

OPERATING INFORMATION

Opening Times: Open at weekends from the 31st March to 24th December and also daily during the school holidays. Open from 10.30am to 6.00pm in the Summer and until 4.30pm at other times.
Steam Working: Steam Weekend – 12th & 13th July
Prices: As a wide variety of rides are available, sheets of ride tickets can be purchased at a rate of £10.00 for 12 tickets or £20.00 for 30 tickets. Each trip on the railway costs 2 ride tickets. Alternatively wristbands which allow unlimited use of all attractions on the day of purchase are also available priced at £15.00 for Children, £10.00 for Adults and £7.50 for Senior Citizens. Group discounts are also available.

Detailed Directions by Car:
From the North: Exit the M1 at Junction 19 and take the A14 towards Kettering. Leave the A14 at Junction 10 and follow signs for Wicksteed Park. Alternatively take the A1 to Stamford, the A43 to Kettering then the A14 as above; From the South: Exit the M1 at Junction 15 and take the A43 to the junction with the A14, then as above. Alternatively take the A1 to the Junction with the A14 then continue to Junction 10 as above.

WINDMILL ANIMAL FARM RAILWAY

Address: Windmill Animal Farm, Red Cat Lane, Burscough L40 1UQ	**Nº of Steam Locos**: 5
Telephone Nº: (07971) 221343	**Nº of Other Locos**: 6
Year Formed: 1997	**Nº of Members**: 7
Location of Line: Burscough, Lancashire	**Annual Membership Fee**: None
Length of Line: 1 mile	**Approx Nº of Visitors P.A.**: 40,000
	Gauge: 15 inches
	Web: www.windmillanimalfarm.co.uk

Photo courtesy of Chris Mansfield

GENERAL INFORMATION

Nearest Mainline Station: Burscough (2½ miles)
Nearest Bus Station: Southport (8½ miles)
Car Parking: Available at the Farm
Coach Parking: Available at the Farm
Souvenir Shop(s): Yes
Food & Drinks: Available

SPECIAL INFORMATION

In addition to the railway, the site includes a play area and a large number of farm animals with a petting area where children can feed the animals.

OPERATING INFORMATION

Opening Times: Open Daily from Easter until mid-September and during weekends and school holidays at all other times. 11.00am to 4.30pm.
Steam Working: Every weekend
Prices: Adult Admission £4.50
Child Admission £3.75
Train Rides: Adult £1.50
Child £1.00

Detailed Directions by Car:
From All Parts: Exit the M6 at Junction 27 and take the A5209 following signs for Southport. On entering Burscough follow signs for Burscough Bridge and Martin Lane. Turn left into Red Cat Lane just by Burscough Bridge train station and follow the road along for Windmill Animal Farm and the Railway.
